ILLUJTRATORJ 43

The Jociety of Illustrators 43rd
Annual of American Illustration

From the exhibition held in the galleries of the
Society of Illustrators Museum of American Illustration
128 East 63rd Street, New York City
March 3 - May 5, 2001

Society of Illustrators, Inc.
128 East 63rd Street, New York, NY 10021-7303
www.societyillustrators.org

While the Society of Illustrators makes every effort possible to publish full and correct
credits for each work included in this volume, sometimes errors of omission or commission may occur.
For this the Society is most regretful, but hereby must disclaim any liability.

As this book is printed in four-color process, a few of the illustrations reproduced here may appear
to be slightly different than in their original reproduction.

ISBN 0-06-008414-6
Library of Congress Catalog Card Number 59-10849

Distributors to the trade in the United States and Canada:

Watson-Guptill Publications
770 Broadway, 8th Floor
New York, NY 10003

Distributors outside the United States and Canada:
HarperCollins International
10 East 53rd Street
New York, NY 10022

Editor, Jill Bossert
Book and jacket design by Bernadette Evangelist
Jacket cover illustration by Richard Krepel

Printed in Hong Kong

Photo Credits: Juliette Borda by Joyce Ravid, Howard Brodie by Brian Lanker,
Dennis Dittrich by Armstrong Photography, Kelly Doe by Larry Fink, Mats Gustafson by Patrik Andersson,
Louise Kollenbaum by Mark Estes, Franklin McMahon by Wm. Franklin McMahon,
Jean Tuttle by Gary Moseson. Photograph of Charles R. Knight's
"Bengal Tiger and Peacock," © Rhoda Steel Kalt
Portrait of Joe Dizney by Nancy Januzzi, portrait of Anita Kunz by John Collier.

ILLUSTRATORS 43

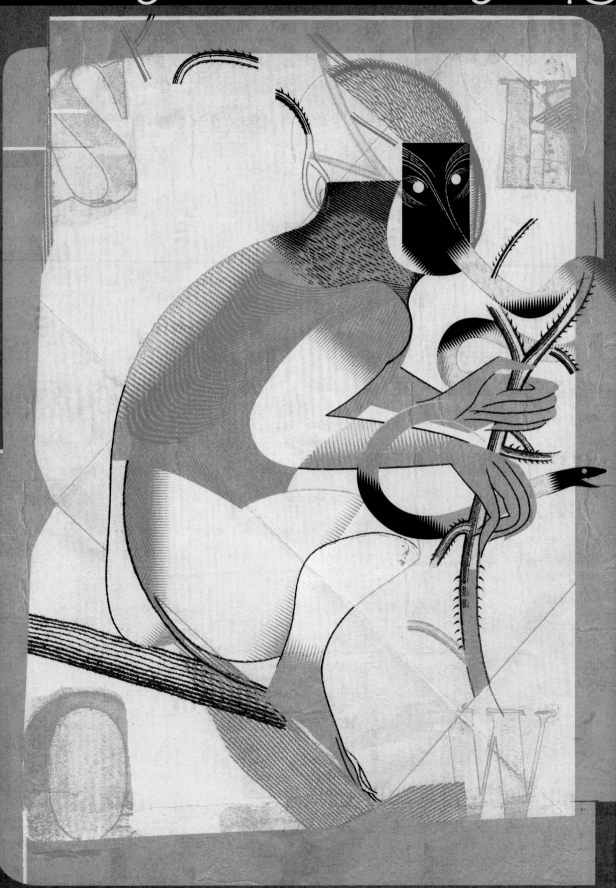

The Society of Illustrators 43rd Annual of American Illustration

CHAIRPERSON'S MESSAGE

I'd like to express my appreciation to a number of people who lent their support and donated their time and talent this past year.

Thank you to Brian Cronin for his poster illustration and to Paul Hardy for the design of the poster and collateral.

Thanks to Joe Ciardiello who was a very involved and much-appreciated assistant chair. Last year's chair, Martha Vaughan, and past president Steven Stroud were both very generous in lending a hand. Thanks to the jurors who demonstrated great dedication.

I'd like to thank Joe Sorren for spontaneously sparking an on-line show of support for the annual.

But most of all a huge thank you goes out to all of the entrants, not just those represented in this book, but to the thousands who keep the desire to be included here alive and thereby make the show possible.

Nancy Stahl

Nancy Stahl
Chairperson,
43rd Annual Exhibition

THE SOCIETY OF ILLUSTRATORS
43RD ANNUAL OF AMERICAN ILLUSTRATION AWARDS GALAS

Left to right: Chairperson Nancy Stahl; Society of Illustrators President Al Lorenz; Erica Sturdevant, Director of Sales and Marketing, American Showcase; and Ann Middlebrook, Executive Vice President, American Showcase, which was once again the Exclusive Sponsor of the Annual Exhibition Awards Galas.

american **showcase**

THE ILLUSTRATORS HALL OF FAME

Since 1958, the Society of Illustrators has elected to its Hall of Fame artists recognized for their "distinguished achievement in the art of illustration." The list of previous winners is truly a "Who's Who" of illustration. Former presidents of the Society meet annually to elect those who will be so honored.

Hall of Fame Laureates 2001

Howard Brodie
Franklin McMahon
John James Audubon*
William H. Bradley*
Felix Octavius Carr Darley*
Charles R. Knight*

Hall of Fame Committee 2001

Chairman, Murray Tinkelman
Chairman Emeritus, Willis Pyle

Former Presidents
Vincent Di Fate
Diane Dillon
Peter Fiore
Charles McVicker
Wendell Minor
Howard Munce
Alvin J. Pimsler
Warren Rogers
Eileen Hedy Schultz
Shannon Stirnweis
John Witt

Hall of Fame Laureates 1958-2000

1958	Norman Rockwell
1959	Dean Cornwell
1959	Harold Von Schmidt
1960	Fred Cooper
1961	Floyd Davis
1962	Edward Wilson
1963	Walter Biggs
1964	Arthur William Brown
1965	Al Parker
1966	Al Dorne
1967	Robert Fawcett
1968	Peter Helck
1969	Austin Briggs
1970	Rube Goldberg
1971	Stevan Dohanos
1972	Ray Prohaska
1973	Jon Whitcomb
1974	Tom Lovell
1974	Charles Dana Gibson*
1974	N.C. Wyeth*
1975	Bernie Fuchs
1975	Maxfield Parrish*
1975	Howard Pyle*
1976	John Falter
1976	Winslow Homer*
1976	Harvey Dunn*
1977	Robert Peak
1977	Wallace Morgan*
1977	J.C. Leyendecker*
1978	Coby Whitmore
1978	Norman Price*
1978	Frederic Remington*
1979	Ben Stahl
1979	Edwin Austin Abbey*
1979	Lorraine Fox*
1980	Saul Tepper
1980	Howard Chandler Christy*
1980	James Montgomery Flagg*
1981	Stan Galli
1981	Frederic R. Gruger*
1981	John Gannam*
1982	John Clymer
1982	Henry P. Raleigh*
1982	Eric (Carl Erickson)*
1983	Mark English
1983	Noel Sickles*
1983	Franklin Booth*
1984	Neysa Moran McMein*
1984	John La Gatta*
1984	James Williamson*
1985	Charles Marion Russell*
1985	Arthur Burdett Frost*
1985	Robert Weaver
1986	Rockwell Kent*
1986	Al Hirschfeld
1987	Haddon Sundblom*
1987	Maurice Sendak
1988	René Bouché*
1988	Pruett Carter*
1988	Robert T. McCall
1989	Erté
1989	John Held Jr.*
1989	Arthur Ignatius Keller*
1990	Burt Silverman
1990	Robert Riggs*
1990	Morton Roberts*
1991	Donald Teague
1991	Jessie Willcox Smith*
1991	William A. Smith*
1992	Joe Bowler
1992	Edwin A. Georgi*
1992	Dorothy Hood*
1993	Robert McGinnis
1993	Thomas Nast*
1993	Coles Phillips*
1994	Harry Anderson
1994	Elizabeth Shippen Green*
1994	Ben Shahn*
1995	James Avati
1995	McClelland Barclay*
1995	Joseph Clement Coll*
1995	Frank E. Schoonover*
1996	Herb Tauss
1996	Anton Otto Fischer*
1996	Winsor McCay*
1996	Violet Oakley*
1996	Mead Schaeffer*
1997	Diane and Leo Dillon
1997	Frank McCarthy
1997	Chesley Bonestell*
1997	Joe DeMers*
1997	Maynard Dixon*
1997	Harrison Fisher*
1998	Robert M. Cunningham
1998	Frank Frazetta
1998	Boris Artzybasheff *
1998	Kerr Eby*
1998	Edward Penfield*
1998	Martha Sawyers*
1999	Mitchell Hooks
1999	Stanley Meltzoff
1999	Andrew Loomis*
1999	Antonio Lopez*
1999	Thomas Moran*
1999	Rose O'Neill*
1999	Adolph Treidler*
2000	James Bama
2000	Alice and Martin* Provensen
2000	Nell Brinkley*
2000	Charles Livingston Bull*
2000	David Stone Martin*
2000	J. Allen St. John*

* Presented posthumously

HOWARD BRODIE

(b. 1915)

"I once wrote that Howard Brodie was the ultimate journalist. I still believe that." Walter Cronkite makes no qualifications in a foreword he contributed for the book *Drawing Fire: The Combat Artist at War*. This collection of Howard Brodie's writings and artwork spans the decades from World War II to Vietnam. Mr. Cronkite, along with many of the "Greatest Generation," first became aware of the powerful artistry of Brodie's work during the Second World War via the Army weekly, *Yank* magazine.

To me, a high school student in the latter part of the 1960s, exposure to Brodie's drawings on the CBS Evening News was the equivalent of a punch to the creative head, and, dare I say, heart. It was an era of notorious trials: Sirhan Sirhan, Charles Manson, My Lai, the Chicago Seven, and Watergate. There on the TV screen, regularly accompanying the court reports, were Howard Brodie's on-the-spot drawings. Brodie's virtuosity stood out as he made quantum leaps in substance and impact which brought pulsating life, palpable dimension, and insight to the personalities and events he portrayed. No doubt many people turned specifically to the CBS Evening News not only to follow the progress of the trials but for the sheer pleasure of marveling at the energy and expressive vibrancy of Brodie's remarkable drawings.

Howard Brodie was born in Oakland, California, in 1915. With pride he lists his educational pedigree at Polytechnic High School in San Francisco, and then at the California School of Fine Arts, the oldest art school in the West. After a stint at the *San Francisco Examiner*, he worked as a full-time sports illustrator with the *San Francisco Chronicle*. World War II brought Brodie to national attention. He enlisted in the Army and signed on as one of over a hundred combat artists for *Yank* magazine, part of the "special forces" who chronicled the war from the enlisted man's point of view. One of *Yank's* best known artists, Brodie chronicled the combat horrors of Guadalcanal with sketchpad, sharp eye, keen memory, and rock solid drawing skills. Running out of his own supplies, Brodie happened upon Prisamcolor wax pencils used by the Navy for mapping

purposes. Using these simple tools, he produced beautiful, strong, brilliant, and unforgettable images, a masterful blend of muscular spontaneity and compassionate insight. Literary giant James Jones, who was stationed in the same war zone, wrote in the book *WWII*, that the drawings Brodie produced from Guadalcanal were a hit everywhere. Brodie went on to record many of the major campaigns of the war in the Pacific and Europe including the Battle of the Bulge, where he was awarded the Bronze Star for "aiding the wounded, and coolness under fire."

After the war, Brodie became a courtroom artist and worked for The Associated Press, CBS News, *Life*, and *Collier's*. He remained close to the military and returned as a combat artist to Korea, French Indochina, and Vietnam. A passionate advocate against the death penalty, he has been witness to and depicted executions. The first was at the Battle of the Bulge, when German soldiers had infiltrated Allied lines posing as GIs. His drawing of a dead German soldier transcends the distinction between "enemy" and "friend" and becomes a universal indictment against premeditated killing.

Throughout his career Brodie has produced drawings of specific events that come to represent more than the image itself. His drawing of Bobby Seale, gagged and strapped to his chair during the trial of the Chicago Seven, speaks as powerfully and eloquently about the spirit of the tumultuous 1960s as the famous poster of Che Guevera. In addition to the drawing of the executed German soldier, there is Brodie's famous "Moving Up" where three GIs on the march come to represent soldiers throughout time. They are exhausted yet relentlessly driven and

grimly determined, with an almost dispassionate will to survive etched in their faces.

Brodie's confidence in his ability is obvious, and his drawing skills are so controlled that even when his line quality is at its wildest, most urgent, and expressionistic, he never loses the sense of structure of his subject. We know the story in the images remains most important. The great jazz master Lester Young once referred to certain saxophonists as "all belly, no brain." Technical prowess, no matter how impressive, without a sense of love and artistic spirit, ultimately adds up to little. Brodie's interest and unquenchable curiosity comes from an expansive love that looks at mankind and embraces its contradictions and ironies, and finds value in even the most horrendous circumstances. He's been a profound witness to this mad past century and has recorded in words and images the best and worst of what he's seen and experienced. Brodie remains a great, generous spirit in spite of a temporary setback from a stroke he suffered several years ago while sketching troops on maneuvers in the Mojave Desert.

The artist's work is in the permanent collections of the Library of Congress, the New Britain Museum of American Art, and the San Francisco Olympic Club. He has been commissioned to draw on movie locations where he worked with Gregory Peck in *Pork Chop Hill*, John Wayne in *The Green Berets*, and Francis Ford Coppola in *Apocalypse Now*. Most recently, film director Terrence Malick sought out Brodie for his visual knowledge of combat for *The Thin Red Line*. Brodie has been blessed with a long, happy marriage to Isabel, also an artist. They are parents both proud and close to their son Bruce and daughter Wendy.

Finally, be it at the San Francisco Academy of Art or at his ranch in central California, Howard Brodie has been an inspired and inspiring teacher to many students, supervising legendary drawing intensives, prodding budding artists to realize through their creative expression that "Love is the heart of life and art."

Victor Juhasz

DOGFACE
PFC MARION D. GRAY
BROWNSVILLE PENN. E.R.

"Dogface," one of a series of sketches covering the Korean War for *Collier's*, 1951.

FRANKLIN McMAHON

(b. 1921)

Born in Chicago in 1921, Franklin McMahon's first artworks were grammar school posters in Beverly Hills, California, and cartoons for his high school newspaper in Oak Park, Illinois. These were the years of the Great Depression so he began marketing his work at an early age, sending batches of drawings to the many magazines that published gag cartoons. To help pay the postage, he sold shares in each batch to his classmates. A major sale to *Collier's* two weeks before graduation in 1939 led to an apprenticeship with an art studio in Chicago.

McMahon attended night school at the Harrison Commercial Art Institute, the American Academy of Art, and the Art Institute of Chicago. He continued to apprentice and do freelance work until World War II when he joined the Naval Air Corps. Later he became a navigator in the Army Air Force and flew B17s over Germany. Shot down at Mannheim, he spent the last months of the war in a prison camp. "[The service] was my last real job," he said. "It didn't work out real well so I went back to freelancing."

In 1945 he and Irene Leahy married and were inseparable for the next fifty-two years until Irene's death in 1997. They attended classes and lectures at Chicago's Institute of Design, and all ideas were discussed at the dinner table. Over the years, nine additional creative chairs were added to that table: five boys and four girls...and, eventually, thirteen grandchildren and two great-grandchildren.

As a designer-illustrator in the early years following the war, McMahon made drawings and laid out pages for *Extension*, *Rotarian*, *Kiwanis*, and other Chicago magazines, ad agencies, and book publishers. Asked to design a book on the Constitution of Illinois by the publisher Row-Peterson, he suggested that he travel throughout the state to make drawings of situations and people affected by that Constitution. Everyone agreed and off he went.

Impressed with the series, the editors of *Life* magazine asked McMahon to report on the Sumner, Mississippi, trial of the men accused of killing Emmitt Till, a teenager from Chicago. Moses Wright, the boy's great-uncle, shook off two hundred years of history when he stood up to point out the men who had come in the night to take the boy. McMahon's drawing was considered by many to be one of the catalysts for the American Civil Rights movement. His coverage of the movement also included the voting rights demonstrations in Selma, Alabama; the Million Man March; and Jesse Jackson's presidential campaigns.

McMahon did two more trials for *Life*, but soon began to feel that the photo magazine would never use him for anything outside the courtroom. If he was going to move on, he would have to do it on his own, initiate his own reports and find a place for them later. He went to Europe to cover the Common Market, and returned for the opening day of Vatican Council II. These portfolios were published by *Fortune*, *The Saturday Evening Post*, *Jubilee*, and *Look*.

Now the phone began to ring and his suggested coverage of goose hunting in Cairo, Illinois, for *Sports Illustrated* led to other assignments including the San Diego-Acapulco yacht race, The Royal Bangkok Sports Club, partridge hunting in Spain, and other stories. His report, "Germany, Twenty

Years Later," ran in the *Chicago Tribune*. His coverage of the Catholic Church includes Pope Paul VI in Jerusalem, and Pope John Paul II's trips to the United States, Mexico, and Poland. Most recently he covered The Parliament of the World's Religions in South Africa, published by *U.S. Catholic* magazine. He had a twelve-year association with Continental Bank, Chicago, reporting on their business affairs in Europe, Asia, Latin America, and Australia. NASA's book, *Eyewitness To Space*, shows twenty McMahon drawings and paintings. He was at Mission Control, Houston, for the first landing on the moon.

In 1960 McMahon did portraits of political figures Adlai Stevenson, Eleanor Roosevelt, and John F. Kennedy. In 1964 he captured Barry Goldwater and Richard Nixon, and began a series on political conventions that has extended to that of George W. Bush in 2000. In 1968 McMahon went to New Hampshire to cover the Eugene McCarthy anti-war movement and ended up amid the chaos of Grant Park in Chicago. This documentary-in-art, which consisted of four hundred drawings and paintings, ran on PBS. Similar programs were made for CBS, Chicago, in 1972, 1976, and 1980, resulting in three Emmys and a Peabody Award.

Irene McMahon was in Selma with her husband and accompanied him to Cape Kennedy. They saw linkage between these two themes that became stories on the new American South. She and their children worked on the films, and she was associate producer of their program reporting on the Chicago Orchestra's 1974 tour of Europe. The McMahons formed a film distribution company called Rocinante Sight & Sound, named for Don Quixote's horse, underlining the spirit of their whole operation. As their children grew Irene became a travel writer and collaborated with Franklin on many stories for international magazines and local newspapers such as *Pioneer Press* in the suburbs of Chicago.

Mark McMahon

Hubert Humphrey wins the 1968 Democratic Party nomination.

JOHN JAMES AUDUBON
(1785-1851)

John James Audubon's name conjures up an image of mythological proportions. Today most people know of the National Audubon Society, but few know much about the man whose name is synonymous with our nation's growing interest in birding and conservation of the environment.

Audubon was born April 26, 1785, on his father's plantation on the Island of Santo Domingo (now known as Haiti). His father, Jean Audubon, was a ship captain, slave-trade merchant, former naval officer, and planter. Although married to a woman in France, the elder Audubon had mistresses on his Santo Domingo plantation. One mistress known only as Mademoiselle Rabin became John James Audubon's mother. His original birth name was given as Fougére, meaning fern. Audubon's birth mother soon died and he was taken to France along with a younger sister from another mistress by their father. Madame Audubon accepted both children as her own, and the young Audubon was formally adopted at age nine. At fifteen, he was baptized and given the name, Jean Jacques Fougére Audubon.

Little is known about young Audubon's education, but it is believed he was taught the basics as well as lessons in fencing, dancing, music, shooting, drawing, and the study of nature.

At eighteen, Audubon's father sent him back to America to avoid service in Napoleon's Army. Young Audubon moved into the comfortable stone house known as Mill Grove near Valley Forge in eastern Pennsylvania. Mill Grove was surrounded by woods and near Perkioming Creek where Audubon first became aquainted with American bird life and where he courted Lucy Bakewell, his wife to be.

In 1806, Audubon started a business partnership, arranged by his father, with Ferdinand Rozier. When Mill Grove was sold, Rozier and Audubon departed for Louisville where they established a retail store and import business. Once established, Audubon

returned to Pennsylvania to marry Lucy Bakewell and bring her west.

Audubon's partnership with Rozier dissolved a few years later, and he became a storekeeper in Henderson, Kentucky. Eventually all of Audubon's business ventures seemed to fall short of expectations including one in New Orleans with his brother-in-law. In 1819 Audubon was jailed for his debts and declared bankruptcy. By this time he had two sons, Victor and John, and two daughters, both of whom died in infancy.

It was during this time that he turned to his artistic talents to eke out a living. Audubon did sign painting and lettering for steamboats and flatboats, and chalk portraits. He also found work at the Western Museum in Cincinnati. There he painted backgrounds and did taxidermy. It was this experience which gave him the courage to strike out on his own.

At age thirty-five Audubon finally made the decision that determined his destiny and forged his legacy.

Up to this point in American history, Alexander Wilson was considered the foremost expert in ornithology. Wilson's nine volume set, *American Ornithology*, was the standard of its day, but Audubon thought that he could do his own edition of all the birds of North America. This turned out to be a task of monumental proportions, the likes of which have never been duplicated.

Audubon, assisted at first by one of his Cincinnati students, Joseph Mason, and later

by his son John, set out on a flatboat down the Ohio river. This adventure would eventually chart some forty thousand miles in search of his avian subjects.

Unable to find an American publisher, Audubon departed for England in 1826 and within two weeks found a willing publisher in London named Robert Havell. Havell turned out to be Audubon's saving grace. Together they created an artistic achievement unequaled in history.

Audubon's *The Birds of North America* (1826-1838) contains 435 hand-colored plates with the birds of America depicted life size. The pages measure twenty-nine and one-half by thirty-nine and one-half inches. These large sheets were known in the printing trade as "double-elephant" giving reference to *The Birds of North America* as the Double Elephant Folio.

Over the ensuing years Audubon struggled to keep his publishing efforts alive by raising money through private subscriptions and turning out numerous paintings for sale.

All in all, some 190 Folios were sold. In addition to the Folios, Audubon produced seven smaller volumes containing a revised version from the *Ornithology Biography*, and in 1845 the first images were produced for *The Viviparous Quadrupeds of North America*. Audubon worked on this project until 1846 when his eyes started to fail and senile dementia began to take hold. *Quadrupeds* was completed by his two sons in 1854. His last days were spent at home along the Hudson River just below the place where George Washington Bridge now stands. Audubon died in 1851 and is buried in Trinity Church Cemetery at 155th Street and Broadway in New York City.

Audubon's contributions to art and to ornithology are now part of our National heritage, and on the 150th anniversary of his passing it is a fitting tribute that he has been elected as a Hall of Fame Laureate.

Wendell Minor

"Great Blue Heron" from *The Birds of America from Drawings Made in the United States and Their Territories*, 1856. Courtesy of Herbert D. Schutz.

WILLIAM H. BRADLEY
(1868-1962)

William H. Bradley, who lived into his nineties, crowded several careers into that long life span. A compulsive worker, from his first job at eleven as a printer's devil for a small newspaper in Ishpening, Michigan, he eventually became one of America's most influential poster artists, printers, and designers.

He was a qualified journeyman printer by thirteen and became a foreman at fifteen. As soon as he was old enough to go on his own, he moved to Chicago to find work as a freelance designer for printers. Self-taught as an artist, he was greatly influenced by Aubrey Beardsley and by the Art Nouveau movement. With a natural flair, he soon found his own drawing style and became conspicuously successful in combining his beautiful pen drawings with typography.

This combination of talents was especially appropriate with the advent of the new poster-craze in the nineties in which Bradley played an important American role, bridging the Art Nouveau and the Arts and Crafts Movements during the latter part of the nineteenth century and the first part of the twentieth. Advertisers vied for his designs, and he also created poster-like conceptions for many manufacturers, including the Chickering Piano Company, Twin Comet Lawn Sprinklers, and Victor Bicycles. For the Worlds Fair of 1894-95, he produced the highly successful booklet, "A Columbia Ode."

Through his own publications, he had a showcase for his ideas and designs that reached to the whole publishing industry. *Bradley: His Book*, self-published quarterly by his Wayside Press, was also designed and published entirely by himself. He changed the layout and design for each issue, and did the artwork and text for most of the ads, which were some of the finest examples of American design of that era. This enormous undertaking, along with his commercial printing jobs, finally resulted in his breakdown in the middle of the fourth number of the second volume when its publication was suspended. Today, complete sets of the volumes are rare collectibles—even the individual ads are prized and framed.

In 1904, Bradley launched a new publication, *The American Chap Book*, which ran for twelve monthly issues, and was based on the eighteenth-century Chap Books, with each issue a different topic—and format. Supplements were printed as broadsides, again displaying the artist's wide-ranging imagination and taste. Type itself was one of his passions. He re-introduced the Caslon face and designed new type faces for American Type Founders, created wallpaper, made pottery designs for Royal Doulton china, designed furniture, a series of Arts and Crafts-styled interiors for *The Ladies' Home Journal*, as well as plans for complete houses to be built for $1,000 to $1,500 (this in 1905). Some of his finest book designs were produced during this time.

He eventually sold his printing plant in 1907, and moved to New York to assume the post of art director for *Collier's* magazine. In the process, Bradley completely revamped its design. He was subsequently hired to do similar re-designs for *Success*, *The Century*, and *Metropolitan* magazines, as well as *Good Housekeeping* and other Hearst publications. He even spent five years—from 1915 to 1920—as art supervisor for several of Hearst-financed movies, one of which he wrote and directed himself. His work is represented in numerous museums including The Metropolitan Museum of Art in New York and the Huntington Library in San Marino, California.

Bradley was able to accomplish so much, carried by the momentum of his enthusiasm. He was an idea man who enjoyed the challenge of new problems and in finding artistic solutions to them. In the process, he employed an elegance and good taste that transcends the limitations of the time in which he worked and that makes his artistry equally eloquent today.

Walt Reed
Founder
Illustration House, Inc.

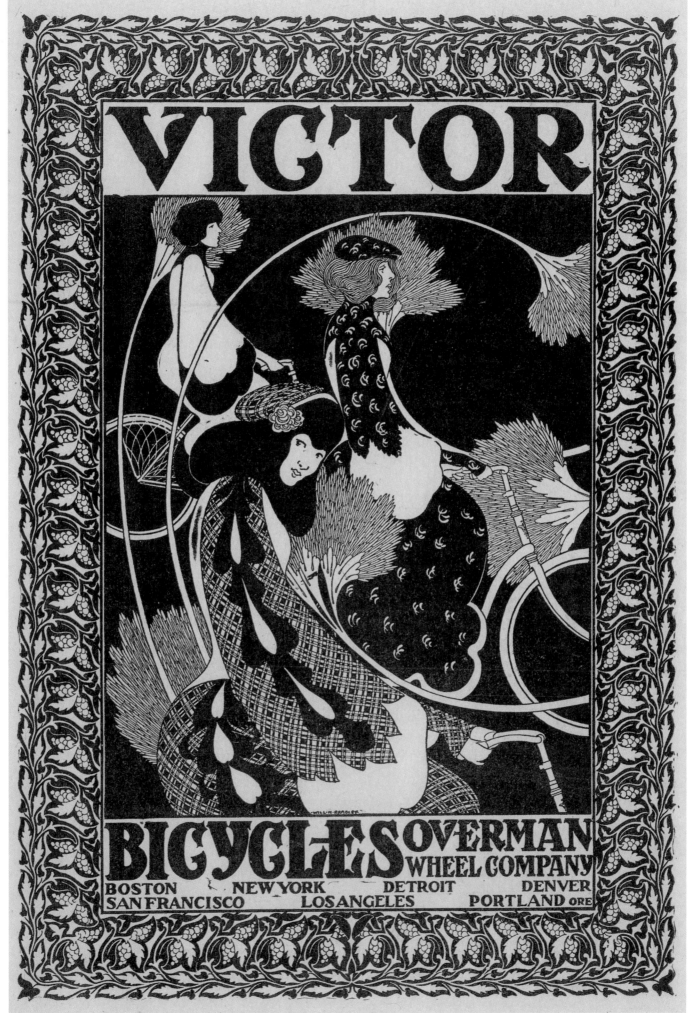

Typical Will Bradley advertising illustration, published in *Harper's Monthly*, February 1896.

FELIX OCTAVIUS CARR DARLEY

(1822-1888)

More than any other single talent, F.O.C. Darley was responsible for the growth of illustration in early America. An article in the *Bulletin of the American Art Union* in August 1851, cites his work as "combining a recognizably sophisticated American point of view with an exceptionally sophisticated style of drawing." The melding of the American viewpoint and his personal style made him the prototype for American illustrators to follow. According to the exhibition catalogue of the 1978 Darley exhibition at the Delaware Art Museum: "Because of his popularity and enormous productivity, Darley's illustrations were the first works of art many Americans experienced." And Henry Pitz, writing in *200 Years of American Illustration*, states: "Darley had no tradition of American illustration behind him. He was himself beginning its creation."

Of course, Darley did not accomplish the burgeoning of American illustration single-handedly—larger sociohistorical forces were involved. Chief among these was a steady rise in the literacy rate. Simultaneously, major technological advances were changing the printing business, allowing more publications with more illustration to be produced at an ever-decreasing cost. Publishing flourished.

Increased visibility made the illustrator a celebrity. Books featured Darley's name as a selling point; soon it became common practice to credit illustrators.

Born in Philadelphia in 1822, Felix O.C. Darley came into a family with strong theatrical roots. Acting interested him, though he showed stronger inclinations toward drawing. At fourteen, Felix became a clerk apprentice with The Philadelphia Dispatch Transportation Line. The budding merchant sketched dockside life on his paperwork. As *The National Magazine* profile of 1856 reported: "Apparently one of his quick sketches of a drunkard attracted the notice of Thomas Dunn English, a prominent writer and critic in Philadelphia. Darley's caricatures found their way to the editor of *The Saturday Museum*,

Edgar Allan Poe, who expressed a desire to publish them."

Once his caricatures appeared in print, Darley's reputation bloomed. By mid-1841, he was hired as staff illustrator for *Graham's Lady's and Gentleman's Magazine*. Soon, however, his horizons broadened and in 1842 he embarked upon a sketching trip to the West, beyond the Mississippi. The trip resulted in his first monumental effort, *Scenes in Indian Life*, which was published in Philadelphia in 1843 to stellar reviews.

As a self-taught artist with little in the way of an established history, Darley did not rely on specific graphic or design-based ideas. He recorded scenes to amplify text or ideas. As such, his illustrations look to us to be disarmingly straightforward and without embellishment or impact.

Working with *The American Art Union*, starting in the late 1840s, Darley created illustrations for a series of prints relating to, yet independent of, classic stories including *Rip van Winkle* and *The Legend of Sleepy Hollow*. The prints were marketed by subscription and became common in upper class homes. Additionally, Darley's talents came into the public's awareness through his impressive output of bank note designs.

In addition, his work appeared in *New York Mercury*—a forerunner of the dime novel which led to the pulp magazine, which, in turn, evolved into the paperback book of today. By the late 1850s, Darley's influence

and reputation had set him head and shoulders above the rest of the field. Yet he never seems to have felt himself superior to any commission and was mainly concerned with keeping his work flourishing with smaller assignments while patiently whittling away at enormous projects.

In 1856, Darley was commissioned to illustrate the complete works of James Fennimore Cooper. These images were reproduced photographically onto the steel die. Prior to this, the appeal and final look of printed illustrations was dependent on the engraver's ability to interpret the artist's tones into incised lines. With the Cooper project, the artistic license of the engraver was essentially eliminated.

Darley was a notoriously dedicated worker throughout his forty-eight years of professional illustrating. The confident assurance that hard work ingrained in Darley is best expressed in the profile published in *The National Magazine*: "One of the first things that strikes you about his sketches is their wonderful clearness of idea. You feel that they are drawn by a ready and skillful hand; one who thoroughly understands himself and his art. He never seems to have hesitated for a moment on the progress of his work. His conception is clear, sharp, and distinct in his mind before he puts pencil to paper. He knows the grouping of every figure, the expression of every face. If he wants a tree in a particular spot, he knows just what species of tree he wants—the size and shape of the bole, the individuality of its bark and moss, every quirl and twist of its boughs, the very twinkle of its leaves. *Nothing is left to chance; all is certainty. He never guesses, he knows.*"

Without his influence, or at least that of another hardworking, talented trailblazer, the Hall of Fame, the Society of Illustrators, and this profession generally, wouldn't exist in America.

Fred Taraba
Director
Illustration House, Inc.

"Zouave." Collection of Carol & Murray Tinkelman.

CHARLES R. KNIGHT
(1874-1953)

Once, eons ago, the ground trembled as great saurian beasts lumbered across a landscape so different from what we know that it looked like the surface of another world. Huge leather-winged creatures glided through purple skies that were gently brushed by the fronds of stunted palms, and colossal funnels of earth spewed lava and smoke into the heavens. Fierce leviathans swam through warm waters, their long necks snaking into the light to snag low-flying pterosaurs or to pluck an Alocodon as it grazed unsuspectingly along the beach. It was a world worthy of Dante, teeming with things more fearsome than all the combined nightmares of every human being who ever dreamed. And it was the genius of Charles R. Knight who gave us our shared vision of these basilisks of an age long lost in time. Much of what we think we know about the look and demeanor of the ancient beings we call dinosaurs we have learned from Knight's authoritative brush, his facile pen and pencil, and his fluid, lifelike sculptures.

A life-long New Yorker, Charles R. Knight was born in Brooklyn on October 21, 1874. Remarkably, an eye injury at age six, complicated by a severe astigmatism, left him legally blind through most of his life. To have sustained such a remarkable career with this handicap alone reveals a dogged predilection toward success and an exceptional strength of will.

Knight received his art education at the Froebel Academy, at Brooklyn's Polytechnic Institute, and at the art school of the Metropolitan Museum of Art before beginning his career at the tender age of 16 with J. & R. Lamb, a firm that specialized in church decoration. With the death of his father two years later, young Charles embarked on a freelance career in illustration that spanned the next six decades and brought him international fame

for his extrapolative paintings of prehistoric animals and of contemporary wildlife. But more than being merely insightful scientific ruminations based on the evidence of Earth's meager fossil records, Knight's paintings are true works of narrative art, introducing to the world at large the story of life and times remote and long past.

Over the course of those years, Knight established a long and fruitful association with the American Museum of Natural History in New York and worked with the likes of Henry Fairfield Osborn and Edward Drinker Cope, pioneering figures in the science of palaeontology. His many murals, paintings, and sculptures are still widely exhibited despite the great changes that have overtaken the field of palaeontology in recent years. And they can be seen at such popular venues as the Bronx Zoo, Chicago's Field Museum, the Natural History Museum of Los Angeles County, the Carnegie Museum in Pittsburgh, and at the Smithsonian Institution's Museum of Natural History and the National Zoo in Washington, D.C.

I first fell in love with dinosaurs, as all young boys inevitably do, at the age of seven. That was in 1953, the year that Charles R. Knight passed away. My love for

them began with a trip to the American Museum of Natural History and with that initial exposure to Knight's magnificent paintings.

At a meeting in New York City in 1983 with the legendary motion picture special effects artist Ray Harryhausen, the subject of Knight's art came up over lunch. Harryhausen (once the protege of Willis O'Brien who created the special effects for the 1933 classic *King Kong*) had studied sculpture for a few years at New York's Art Students League. While living in Manhattan, Harryhausen looked up Knight's address in the phone book and made a ritual of lingering outside his studio on West 67th Street in the hope of having a "chance" meeting with the painter who had so influenced his life. Although Harryhausen observed Knight's daily comings and goings, he could never quite summon the courage to approach him. Ray Harryhausen would become a titan of the film industry with his work on such notable dinosaur movies as *The Beast from 20,000 Fathoms* (1953), *The Animal World* (1955), *One Million Years B.C.* (1966), and *Valley of Gwangi* (1969).

His shyness in the presence of Charles Knight was revealing, both of Harryhausen's retiring and very human nature and of the awe in which he and so many of the rest of us—no matter how accomplished—hold the true giants of illustration's royalty.

It is a feat to create captivating narrative paintings using the traditional tools of illustration, but it is something so much more to take limited information and build from it a world so unknown to us and yet so thoroughly convincing in its detail that we come to accept it without reservation. Such was the scope of Knight's magnificent talent—a talent for which the child in each of us will be eternally grateful.

Vincent Di Fate

"Bengal Tiger and Peacock." Courtesy of Rhoda Steel Kalt.

THE HAMILTON KING AWARD 2001

JAMES BENNETT

(b. 1960)

The Hamilton King Award, created by Mrs. Hamilton King in memory of her husband through a bequest, is presented annually for the best illustration of the year by a member of the Society. The selection is made by former recipients of this award and may be won only once.

———

Jim Bennett is tired of constantly being asked the same question: Do you work with an airbrush?

And I'm tired of constantly answering the same question: Do you really know Jim Bennett?

The answer to the second question is yes, we are well acquainted. Jim is quite unaware of the fact, but I sought him out to prove a point. Richard Solomon had, by way of Chris Payne, sent me some samples of Jim's work, looking for my opinion. My first reaction upon seeing the technical virtuosity was to utter an unbroken string of every curse word I knew and a couple that I have made up for just such occasions. My next reaction was to ask if he was working with an airbrush. When I found out the answer was "no" I started cursing again.

My third reaction was the strongest. There was something within these paintings which told me that, were we ever to meet, I would like the artist. My only explanation for this feeling is the fact that Jim's work exudes—and this is one of the most undervalued words in today's society—niceness.

It is not cloying or saccharine niceness, but a fair-mindedness for his subject matter. I'm never sure if this is a conscious decision of the artist or one thrust upon him by the sub-conscious but, today, choosing nice over cynical is the tougher road. This is not to say that nice guys finish last—this award alone

has disproven that cliché—but they sure don't always get the choicest assignments.

I also believe it is the tougher road aesthetically. It is one of the unfortunate truths of the universe, whether we are speaking physically, spiritually, or artistically, that it is easier to push a man down than to help lift him up.

I believe that Jim's brush helps elevate each subject it rests upon.

And so, as I said, I sought him out to prove a point to myself and I did. The artist is as pleasant as his work. Mind you, when two illustrators set out to become friends, there are always a couple of obstacles but, as luck would have it, our wives did like each other so it was clear sailing.

Of Jim's early life growing up in South Jersey (Abselon to be precise), I can speak with no authority. But there are rumors. Even to hear Jim tell it, at one point it was a toss-up as to whether or not a Jim Bennett picture would hang in an art gallery or the post office. I personally find this difficult to believe. The Jim I have gotten to know is a model father to Steven and Brett, a model husband to Susan and, in general, a model citizen. (Mind you, if you look up the word "model"

in the dictionary, one definition is "a small version of the real thing," so who knows?)

Jim started his artistic schooling at Bucks County Community College and then, with the aid of a scholarship, found himself at the School of Visual Arts. It was there that Jim took a class instructed by Society of Illustrators perennial favorite Michael Deas. It was one assignment in particular for Michael that Jim credits with altering his own vision of his work. The idea was to take a painting by a Dutch master and break it down into a grid. You then took the grid and distorted it as much as you liked. The end result demonstrated to Jim some untested boundaries that he is still exploring.

As I write these words, I need only look to my left in my studio to see the fruits of his explorations. It is my own original Bennett. It is painted with such unabashed joy that it cannot help but bring joy to the viewer. It answers that first question nicely. Jim Bennett doesn't use an airbrush. The canvas I'm looking at is a swirling sea of thick creamy oils showing extreme meticulousness in places, wild abandonment in others. But a Jim Bennett is not about simple technique. The second sphere of joy is the subject matter. In this picture one sees a rendition of the famous shot from the film *Titanic*: an upward angle at dusk with two figures leaning over the bow, arms outstretched. In this particular case, however, we find Winslet and DiCaprio replaced by Bill Clinton and Monica Lewinsky.

This could have been a savaging of both subjects. Instead, there is charm, humor, and intelligence—the three words I think of when I think of Jim Bennett.

Mark Summers

"Scratch."

JURY

Betsy Lewin, Chair
Children's book illustrator

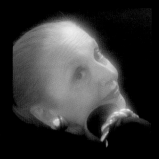

Terry Allen
Illustrator

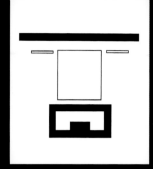

Elaine Duillo
Illustrator

Mark Friedman
Executive Vice President
Creative Director
Cline, Davis & Mann

Robin Gilmore-Barnes
Art Director
The Atlantic Monthly

Steven Guarnaccia
Illustrator/Designer

Victor Juhasz
Illustrator

Amy Ning
Illustrator

Mitch Shostak
Principal
Shostak Studios Inc.

1 Gold Medal
Artist: **Brian Cronin**
Art Directors: Geraldine Hessler
Robert Festino
Client: Entertainment Weekly
Medium: India ink, acrylic on paper

Brian Cronin was engaged to illustrate a story in *Entertainment Weekly* about writers and heredity. Can great literary skill be passed down through generations? "I like to keep things simple. In this case I used the color of ink to tell the story of looking for the family tree. I like the link between the color of the ink and the color of blood, blue and red."

2 Gold Medal
Artist: **Mats Gustafson**
Art Director: Christine Curry
Client: The New Yorker
Medium: Ink

Swedish artist Mats Gustafson studied stage design at the National College of Fine Art in Stockholm. His first commission was from *British Vogue* in 1978, and his work frequently appears in leading fashion magazines worldwide. He maintains editorial collaborations with *Vogue Italia*, *The New Yorker*, and *Visionaire*. His advertising clients include Bergdorf Goodman, Chanel, Esteé Lauder, Tiffany & Co., Calvin Klein, Burberry, Romeo Gigli, and Yohji Yamamoto. His drawings have been exhibited in Sweden, France, Germany, and Japan.

3 Silver Medal
Artist: **Steve Brodner**
Art Director: Steven Heller
Client: The New York Times Book Review
Medium: Watercolor on watercolor paper
Size: 20" h x 15" w

Steve Brodner has been a cartoonist, satiric illustrator, and art journalist for publications since, well, way back. His pictures, which have been in most major magazines, have attempted to nail various political and corporate nitwits. His work has been appreciated by public figures who think that damning caricatures of themselves is some kind of badge of honor, by college kids who allow it to mislead them about what you can get away with in illustration, and by art directors (bless them) who don't mind putting their jobs at risk by including illustration that tries to say some true things. He has been a devoted member of the Society of Illustrators for 22 years and is very grateful for his medal.

4 Silver Medal
Artist: **Arnold Roth**
Art Director: Christine Curry
Client: The New Yorker

"I am a freelance cartoonist. My work has appeared in many publications: *Punch*, *The New Yorker*, *Sports Illustrated*, *Esquire*, and *Playboy* being among the notable ones of the many hundreds. Syndicated comics, children's books, animation, etc., have all been polluted by my efforts. An exhibition marking my 50th year as a freelancer commenced in the autumn of 2001 and will eventually be displayed at the Society of Illustrators Museum of American Illustration in the fall of 2002."

5 Silver Medal
Artist: **Jack Unruh**
Art Director: Danielle LeBel
Client: En Route
Medium: Ink, watercolor on board
Size: 13" h x 11" w

"Boy, howdy!. . .Gee whiz! . . . This is fun! The fishing and the picture drawing. I love the opportunity to do both and the business of illustration makes it possible. A very special thanks to those clients who hire us and give us the freedom to do our work. Pretty good fish, huh?"

6 Silver Medal
Artist: **Andrea Ventura**
Art Director: Michael Lawton
Client: Men's Journal
Medium: Mixed on paper

The sports world's all-star New York Knick guard was a total stranger to Ventura, who doesn't follow sports. "It doesn't always help to know the person, as I mostly concentrate on the eyes and the expression." He hinted at the team's logo and presented the blue and orange team colors intentionally out of focus. The effect is a careful yet powerful likeness.

7
Artist: **Marshall Arisman**
Art Director: Leanne Shapton
Client: National Post
Medium: Oil on ragboard
Size: 29" h x 22" w

8
Artist: **Jeffrey Decoster**
Art Director: Jim Nelson
Client: Minneapolis/St. Paul Magazine

9
Artist: **Gerard DuBois**
Art Director: Andrew Capitos
Client: Red Herring Magazine
Size: 11" h x 8" w

10
Artist: **James McMullan**
Art Director: Steven Heller
Client: The New York Times Book Review
Medium: Watercolor on paper
Size: 7" h x 9" w

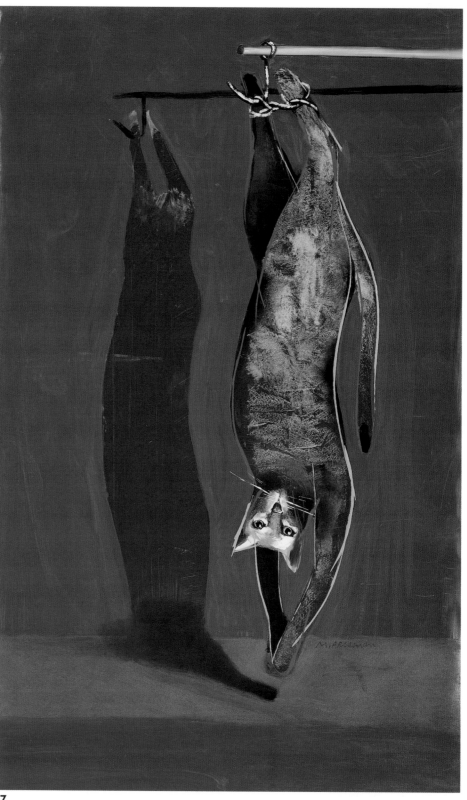

7

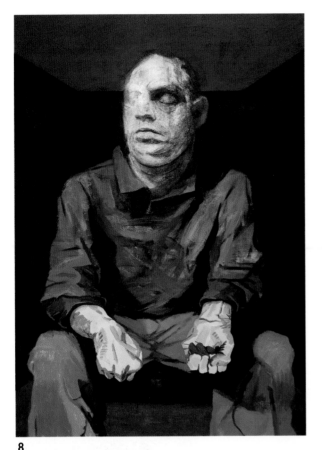

8

9

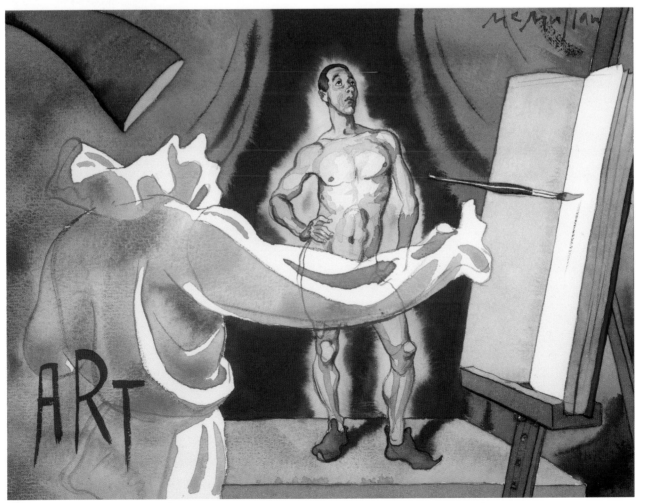

10

11
Artist: **Jeffrey Smith**
Art Director: Jessica Power
Client: New York Magazine
Medium: Watercolor on paper
Size: 7" h x 5" w

12
Artist: **Jeffrey Smith**
Art Director: Robin Gilmore-Barnes
Client: The Atlantic Monthly
Medium: Watercolor on paper
Size: 5" h x 10" w

13
Artist: **Dave McKean**
Art Director: Nick Torello
Client: Penthouse

14
Artist: **Robert Meganck**
Art Director: Jandos Rothstein
Client: Washington City Paper
Medium: Digital
Size: 10" h x 7" w

11

12

13

14

15
Artist: **James McMullan**
Art Director: Leanne Shapton
Client: Saturday Night
Medium: Watercolor on paper
Size: 10" h x 8" w

16
Artist: **Mike Benny**
Art Director: Tom Staebler
Client: Playboy
Medium: Acrylic
Size: 15" h x 16" w

17
Artist: **Jeffrey Smith**
Art Director: Robin Gilmore-Barnes
Client: The Atlantic Monthly
Medium: Watercolor on paper
Size: 8" h x 11" w

18
Artist: **Jim Burke**
Art Director: Andrew Kner
Client: Scenario Magazine
Medium: Oil on board
Size: 14" h x 23" w

15

16

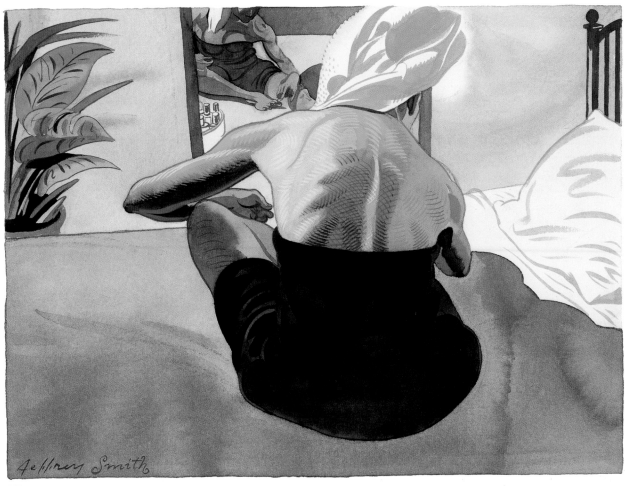

17

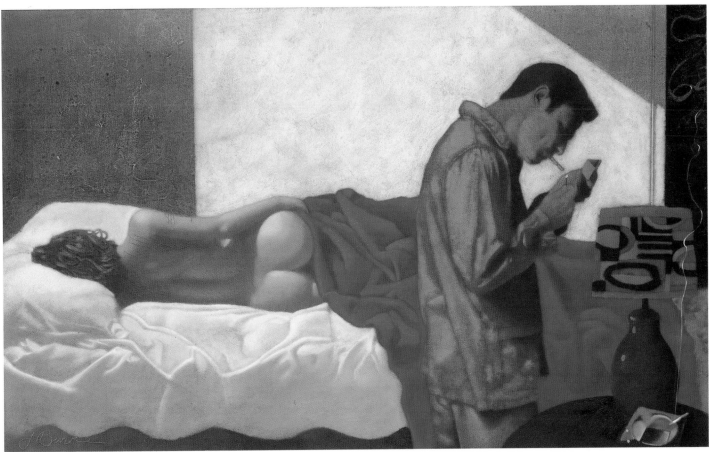

18

19
Artist: **Kinuko Y. Craft**
Art Director: Tom Staebler
Client: Playboy

20
Artist: **Gary Kelley**
Art Director: Fred Woodward
Client: Rolling Stone
Medium: Pastel on paper

21
Artist: **Robert Risko**
Art Director: Fred Woodward
Client: Rolling Stone

22
Artist: **Daniel Adel**
Art Director: John Korpics
Client: Esquire
Medium: Oil on board

23
Artist: **Daniel Adel**
Art Directors: Geraldine Hessler
　　　　　　　Jennifer Procopio
Client: Entertainment Weekly
Medium: Oil on canvas

24
Artist: **Anita Kunz**
Art Director: Francoise Mouly
Client: The New Yorker
Medium: Mixed on board

19

20

21

22

23

24

25
Artist: **Edel Rodriguez**
Art Director: Michael Mrak
Client: TIME Custom Publishing
Medium: Pastel, woodblock ink on paper
Size: 9" h x 7" w

26
Artist: **Robert Grossman**
Art Director: Fred Woodward
Client: Rolling Stone

27
Artist: **Victor Juhasz**
Art Director: Fran Fiefield
Client: Fortune Magazine
Medium: Pen & ink, watercolor on paper
Size: 17" h x 21"

28
Artist: **Jack Unruh**
Art Director: Scott Dadich
Client: Texas Monthly
Medium: Ink, watercolor on board
Size: 18" h x 13" w

29
Artist: **Anita Kunz**
Art Directors: Geraldine Hessler
              Joe Kimberling
Client: Entertainment Weekly
Medium: Mixed on board

25

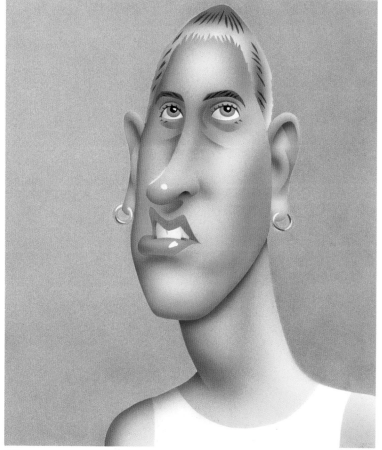

26

27

28

29

30
Artist: **Mark Ryden**
Art Director: Geraldine Hessler
Client: Entertainment Weekly

31
Artist: **Roberto Parada**
Art Director: Robin Gilmore-Barnes
Client: The Atlantic Monthly
Medium: Oil on canvas
Size: 16" h x 12" w

32
Artist: **Roberto Parada**
Art Director: Rockwell Harwood
Client: Esquire
Medium: Oil on canvas
Size: 14" h x 18" w

33
Artist: **Tim O'Brien**
Art Director: Deanna Lowe
Client: Worth Magazine
Medium: Oil on panel
Size: 13" h x 9" w

34
Artist: **Roberto Parada**
Art Director: Nick Torello
Client: Penthouse
Medium: Oil on canvas

30

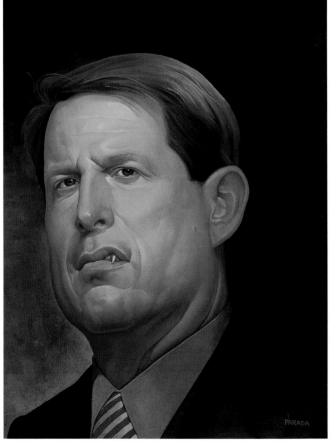

31

32

33

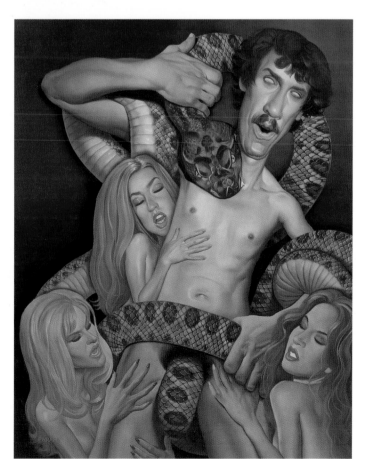

34

35
Artist: **Al Hirschfeld**
Client: The New Yorker

36
Artist: **John Kascht**
Art Director: Teresa Fernandes
Client: Talk Magazine
Medium: Colored ink, watercolor on
         Strathmore Bristol
Size: 12" h x 20" w

37
Artist: **Ruth Marten**
Art Director: Richard Baker
Client: Premiere

38
Artist: **John Kascht**
Art Director: Richard Baker
Client: Premiere

35

36

37

38

39

Artist: **Al Hirschfeld**

Art Director: Fred Woodward

Client: Rolling Stone

40

Artist: **Edward Sorel**

Art Director: Owen Phillips

Client: The New Yorker

Medium: Pen & ink, watercolor on
mounted bond paper

Size: 26" h x 21" w

41

Artist: **Joe Ciardiello**

Art Director: Nancy McMillen

Client: Texas Monthly

Medium: Pen & ink, watercolor on paper

Size: 23" h x 19" w

39

40

42
Artist: **Joe Ciardiello**
Art Directors: Fred Woodward
Gail Anderson
Client: Rolling Stone
Medium: Pen & ink, watercolor on paper
Size: 19" h x 14" w

43
Artist: **Mark Ulriksen**
Art Director: Fred Woodward
Client: Rolling Stone

44
Artist: **Andrea Ventura**
Art Director: Steven Heller
Client: The New York Times Book Review
Medium: Mixed on paper
Size: 20" h x 16" w

45
Artist: **Riber Hansson**
Client: Sovenska Dagbladet
Medium: Acrylic, oil on linen
Size: 58 cm h x 63 cm w

43

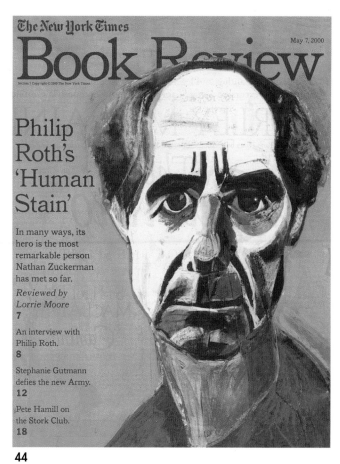

44

45

46
Artist: **Tim O'Brien**
Art Directors: Marti Golon
                     Arthur Hochstein
Client: TIME
Medium: Oil on panel
Size: 13" h x 18" w

47
Artist: **Peter Sylvada**

48
Artist: **M. Christopher Zacharow**
Art Director: Robin Gilmore-Barnes
Client: The Atlantic Monthly
Medium: Acrylic on canvas board
Size: 20" h x 16" w

49
Artist: **Anita Kunz**
Art Director: Jen Procopio
Client: Entertainment Weekly
Medium: Mixed on board

50
Artist: **Marco Ventura**
Art Director: Giovanni Sammarco
Client: Amica
Medium: Oil on paper
Size: 9" h x 8" w

46

47

49

48

50

51
Artist: **Kinuko Y. Craft**
Art Director: Sharon Okamoto
Client: TIME
Medium: Gouache on paper
Size: 11" h x 8" w

52
Artist: **Rob Day**
Art Director: Ed Rich
Client: Smithsonian
Medium: Oil on paper

53
Artist: **Jody Hewgill**
Art Director: Shauna Wolf Narciso
Client: Amazing Stories
Medium: Acrylic on gessoed board
Size: 9" h x 18" w

54
Artist: **Brett Helquist**
Art Director: Ron McCutchan
Client: Cricket
Medium: Oil, acrylic on paper
Size: 13" h x 20" w

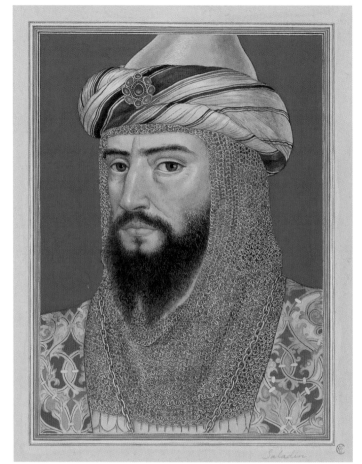

51

52

53

55

Artist: **Marc Burckhardt**

Art Director: Robin Gilmore-Barnes

Client: The Atlantic Monthly

Medium: Acrylic on wood

Size: 14" h x 10" w

56

Artist: **Dugald Stermer**

Art Director: Steven Heller

Client: The New York Times Book Review

Medium: Pencil, watercolor on Arches paper

Size: 16" h x 20" w

57

Artist: **Jody Hewgill**

Art Directors: Kevin Fisher
          Isabel De Sousa

Client: Audubon Magazine

Medium: Acrylic on gessoed board

Size: 13" h x 9" w

58

Artist: **Max Grafe**

Art Directors: Kevin Fisher
          Isabel De Sousa

Client: Audubon Magazine

Medium: Mixed on handmade paper

Size: 23" h x 23" w

59

Artist: **Jason Holley**

Art Director: Laura Zavetz

Client: Bloomberg Wealth
          Manager Magazine

55

56

57

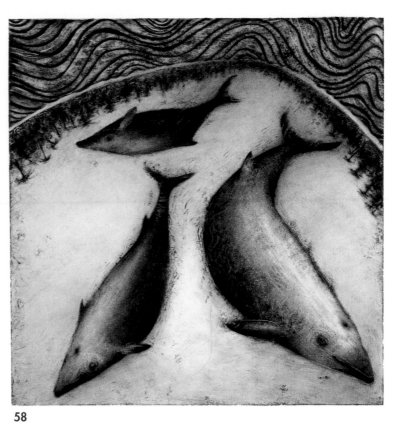

58

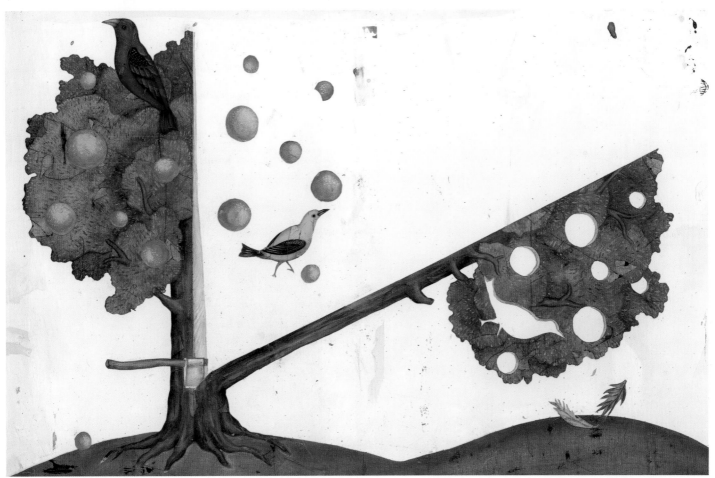

59

60
Artist: **Eric Westbrook**
Art Director: Karen Pauls
Client: Concordia Publishing
Medium: Acrylic on canvas
Size: 10" h x 10" w

61
Artist: **Ricardo Martinez**
Art Director: Carmelo Caderot
Client: El Mundo
Medium: Scratchboard
Size: 9" h x 11" w

62
Artist: **Edward Sorel**
Art Director: Francoise Mouly
Client: The New Yorker
Medium: Pen & ink, watercolor on
          mounted bond paper
Size: 26" h x 21" w

63
Artist: **Peter de Sève**
Art Director: Francoise Mouly
Client: The New Yorker
Medium: Watercolor, ink on
          watercolor paper
Size: 15" h x 10" w

64
Artist: **Jason Holley**
Art Director: John Korpics
Client: Esquire

65
Artist: **Dugald Stermer**
Art Director: Cynthia Hoffman
Client: TIME
Medium: Pencil, watercolor on
          Arches paper
Size: 20" h x 16" w

60

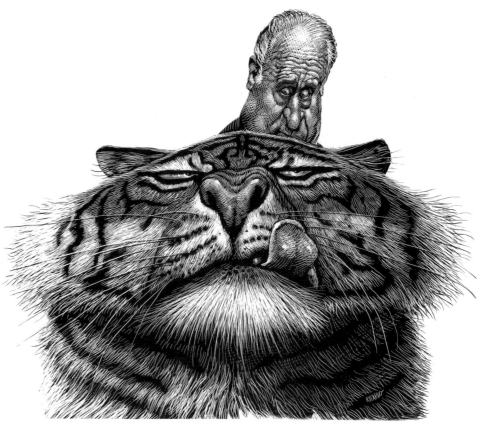

61

62

63

64

65

66

Artist: **Adam Niklewicz**

Art Director: Gillian Kahn

Client: American Recorder

Medium: Acrylic on board

Size: 12" h x 10" w

67

Artist: **Tim Bower**

Art Directors: John Korpics
                 Erin Whelan

Client: Esquire

Size: 14" h x 18" w

68

Artist: **Jack Unruh**

Art Director: Dave Cox

Client: Outside Magazine

Medium: Ink, watercolor on board

Size: 19" h x 27" w

69

Artist: **Brian Cronin**

Art Directors: Geraldine Hessler
                 Robert Festino

Client: Entertainment Weekly

70

Artist: **Guy Billout**

Art Directors: Kevin Fisher
                 Isabel De Sousa

Client: Audubon Magazine

Medium: Watercolor, airbrush on
          Bristol vellum

Size: 6" h x 4" w

66

67

68

69

70

71
Artist: **C.F. Payne**
Art Director: Steve Hoffman
Client: Sports Illustrated
Medium: Mixed on board

72
Artist: **Kadir Nelson**
Art Director: Roseanne Berry
Client: Sports Illustrated
Medium: Oil on canvas
Size: 24" h x 30" w

73
Artist: **David Ho**
Art Director: Miguel Riviera
Client: The Source Sports
Medium: Digital

74
Artist: **Tim Zeltner**
Art Director: Jackie Shipley
Client: Today's Grandparent Magazine
Medium: Acrylic on wood
Size: 16" h x 12" w

71

72

73

74

75
Artist: **Philippe Weisbecker**
Art Director: Patty Alvarez
Client: The Boston Sunday Globe
Medium: Mixed

76
Artist: **Nicholas Wilton**
Art Director: Guiv Rahbar
Client: Yoga Journal

77
Artist: **Nicholas Wilton**
Art Director: Martha Geering
Client: Sierra Magazine

78
Artist: **Philippe Weisbecker**
Art Director: Melanie DeForest
Client: Fast Company
Medium: Mixed on paper

76

77

78

79
Artist: **Steven Guarnaccia**
Art Director: Michael Valenti
Client: The New York Times
Medium: Pen & ink, watercolor on paper

80
Artist: **Daniel Zakroczemski**
Art Director: John Davis
Client: Buffalo News
Medium: Pastel on paper
Size: 15" h x 11" w

81
Artist: **Brad Yeo**
Art Director: Meg Birnbaum
Client: American Prospect Magazine
Medium: Acrylic on canvas
Size: 22" h x 16" w

82
Artist: **Tim Clark**
Art Director: Sarah Hollander
Client: Mortgage Bankers Association
        of America
Medium: Gouache, watercolor on
            Arches paper
Size: 11" h x 8" w

79

80

81

82

83

Artist: **Benoit**

Client: The New Yorker

84

Artist: **Raúl Colón**

Art Director: Francoise Mouly

Client: The New Yorker

Medium: Watercolor, colored
pencil on paper

Size: 16" h x 12" w

85

Artist: **Guy Billout**

Art Director: Robin Gilmore-Barnes

Client: The Atlantic Monthly

Medium: Watercolor, airbrush on
Bristol vellum

Size: 9" h x 7" w

86

Artist: **Chris Gall**

Art Director: Gary Kelley

Client: North American Review

Medium: Scratchboard, dye on paper

Size: 14" h x 10" w

87

Artist: **Gene Greif**

Art Director: Leah Purcell

Client: Newsweek

Medium: Acrylic, crayon on Bristol board

Size: 9" h x 7" w

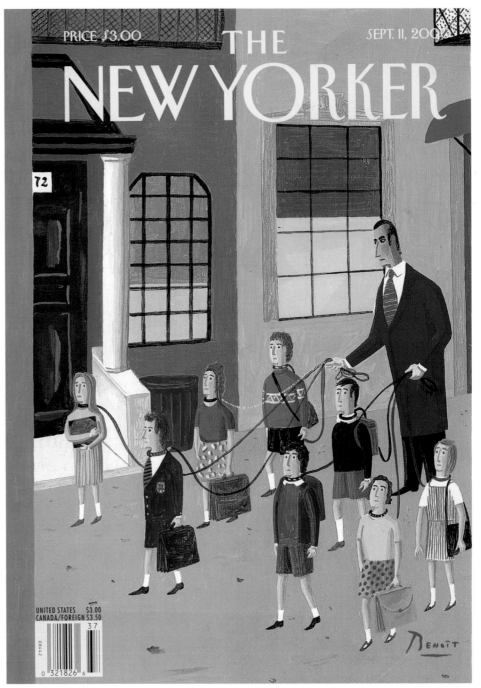

84

85

86

87

88

Artist: **Jim Frazier**

Art Directors: Robert Mansfield
Anton Klusener

Client: Forbes

89

Artist: **Robert Neubecker**

Art Director: Kathleen Kincaid

Client: Slate

Medium: Ink

Size: 11" h x 8" w

90

Artist: **Edel Rodriguez**

Art Director: Owen Phillips

Client: The New Yorker

Medium: Pastel, colored pencil on paper

Size: 7" h x 12" w

91

Artist: **Brian Cronin**

Art Directors: Geraldine Hessler
Robert Festino

Client: Entertainment Weekly

92

Artist: **Brian Cronin**

Art Directors: Geraldine Hessler
Erin Whelan

Client: Entertainment Weekly

88

89

90

91

92

93

Artist: **Craig Frazier**
Art Director: Daphne Nash
Client: Wink Magazine
Medium: Digital
Size: 26" h x 22" w

94

Artist: **Craig Frazier**
Art Director: Daphne Nash
Client: Wink Magazine
Medium: Digital
Size: 26" h x 22" w

95

Artist: **Jeffrey Fisher**
Art Director: Frank Tagariello
Client: Bloomberg Personal
Medium: Acrylic on paper

96

Artist: **Leo Espinosa**
Art Director: Tom Staebler
Client: Playboy
Medium: Digital

97

Artist: **Jean-Manuel Duvivier**
Art Director: Sandro Occhipinti
Client: L'Espresso Magazine
Medium: Colored papers
Size: 19 cm h x 18 cm w

93

94

95

96

97

98
Artist: **Steven Guarnaccia**
Art Director: Gail Anderson
Client: Rolling Stone
Medium: Pen & ink, watercolor on paper

99
Artist: **Ross MacDonald**
Art Directors: Robert Mansfield
                    Charles Brulaliere
Client: Forbes

100
Artist: **Christian Northeast**
Art Director: Tom Staebler
Client: Playboy

101
Artist: **Tim Bower**
Art Director: Hannu Laakso
Client: Reader's Digest

98

99

100

101

102

Artist: **Leo Espinosa**
Art Director: Patrick Prince
Client: Internet World
Medium: Digital

103

Artist: **Mark Alan Stamaty**
Art Director: Steven Heller
Client: The New York Times Book Review
Medium: Mixed on Strathmore (plate finish)

104

Artist: **Peter de Sève**
Art Director: Francoise Mouly
Client: The New Yorker
Medium: Watercolor, ink on
        watercolor paper
Size: 15" h x 11" w

105

Artist: **Charles Burns**
Art Directors: Geraldine Hessler
        Tracy Walsh
Client: Entertainment Weekly

102

103

104

105

106
Artist: **Lasse Skarbovik**
Client: Visuelt Magazine
Medium: Digital

107
Artist: **Terry Allen**
Art Director: Laura Zavetz
Client: Bloomberg Wealth
Manager Magazine

108
Artist: **Adam McCauley**
Art Director: Gillian Kahn
Client: American Recorder
Medium: Mixed on watercolor paper

109
Artist: **Lou Myers**
Art Director: Francis Tenabe
Client: Washington Post Book World

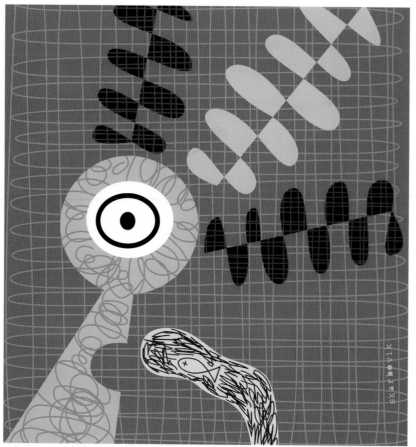

106

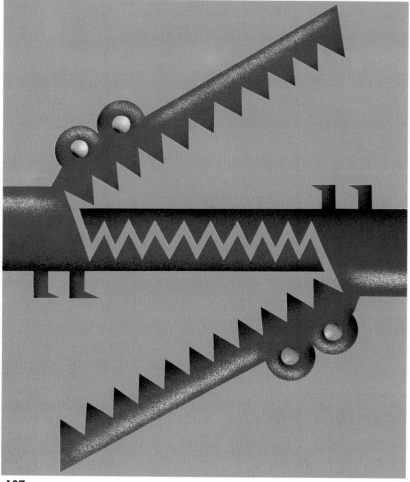

107

108

BOOK

JURY

Marshall Arisman, Chair
Illustrator

Harriett Barton
*Creative Director/Hardcover
Books HarperCollins
Children's Books*

Juliette Borda
Illustrator

Bill Harbort
Illustrator/Educator

Louise Kollenbaum
*Product Development/Art
Direction/Consulting*

Tim Lewis
Illustrator

James Ransome
Illustrator

James Yang
Illustrator

110 Gold Medal
Artist: **Tomer Hanuka**
Client: Meathaus Press
Medium: Ink, digital
Size: 8" h x 5" w

"This piece was done for the cover of *Meathaus*, a comic anthology featuring work by young, alternative artists. I tried to depict a certain awkwardness that comes with being outside the cultural mainstream. It's a blessed awkwardness really, since it embodies the freedom of being exactly who you are. The kid in the center of the piece is Ink Stains Louis, a circus freak who runs away when a doctor comes to "heal" his special skin condition. The anthology is edited by Farel Dalrymple, who gave me the opportunity to do a cover, and the liberty to do whatever I felt was right. The award from the Society came as a complete shock. I am very grateful for being part of this amazing collection."

111 Gold Medal
Artist: **Andrea Ventura**
Art Director: Gary Gifford
Client: Houghton Mifflin Company
       McDougal Littell
Medium: Mixed on paper
Size: 20" h x 16" w

This portrait of the late Jorge Luis Borges, one of Argentina's most important writers, is one of a series of five famous South American literati for Houghton Mifflin for use as high school texts. "Mr. Borges has a very interesting face, and the fact that he is in the arts makes the job easier as well." Ventura maintains his own reference archives and found just what he was looking for in the charismatic, blind writer.

112 Silver Medal
Artist: **Greg Clarke**
Art Director: Angela Carlino
Client: Atheneum Books for Young Readers
Medium: Acrylic on board
Size: 9" h x 6" w

"I prefer to let the concept and composition dictate the medium I use. I usually work in watercolor, but the simplicity of this composition seemed to call for something more painterly. I was fortunate to be working with Angela Carlino, a designer who trusted me to use acrylic even though she was only familiar with my watercolor work. I am an illustrator based in Los Angeles who contributes to *The Atlantic Monthly, Entertainment Weekly, Time, Rolling Stone,* and elsewhere."

113 Silver Medal
Artist: **Geneviève Côté**
Art Director: Diane Primeau
Client: Dominique & Friends Publishers
Medium: Mixed
Size: 7" h x 7" w

"Over the last ten years, I have illustrated for various publications (*The Boston Globe, The New York Times, Utne Reader,* and many others) on a variety of topics ranging from the serious to the funny or the frankly bizarre. I still love it. Recently, I fell in love with children's literature. Seeing kids' drawings of fish, inspired by *The Little Black Sheep,* or hearing them say they bring my ogre *L'Affreux* to bed every night is a new and quite addictive feeling. I am very happy that these illustrations have also appealed to the jury of the Society of Illustrators, and proud to be part of *Illustrators 43,* among so many talented artists."

114 Silver Medal
Artist: **Tomer Hanuka**
Client: Bipolar
Medium: Ink, digital
Size: 8" h x 5" w

"This illustration was created for the cover of *Bipolar*. The book features the work of my twin brother Assaf and myself. We live very far apart, and sometimes the closest I can get to him will be to look in the mirror." Tomer Hanuka was born in Israel in 1974 and grew up surrounded by American comic books. He moved to New York in 1996 and received his BFA from the School of Visual Arts. His work has appeared in various magazines and he creates his own comic books. He believes that visual narrative can change the world, and rock and roll can't.

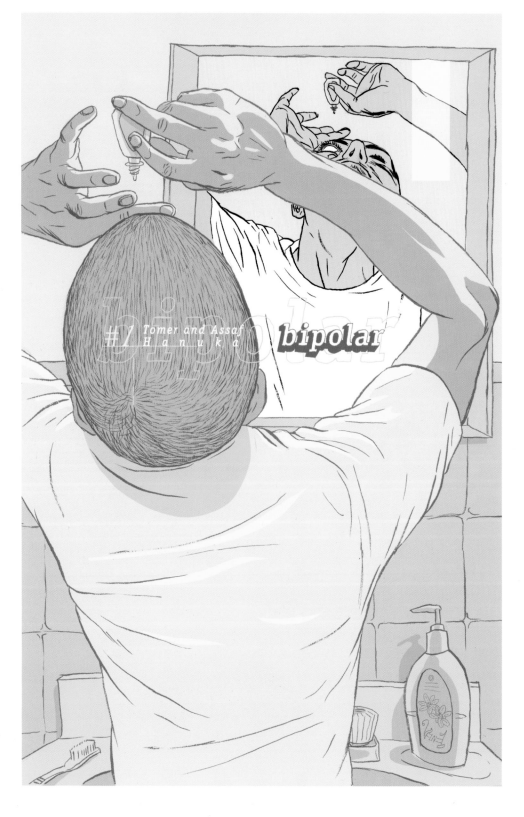

115 Silver Medal
Artist: **Nina Laden**
Art Director: Kristen Nobles
Client: Chronicle Books
Medium: Collage, cut paper

Born in New York City in 1962, and graduated from Syracuse University with a BFA in Illustration in 1983, Nina Laden has worked as an illustrator ever since. She also writes children's books. In 1994, her first book, *The Night I Followed the Dog,* was an award-winning success. Eight more books and many awards have followed. This illustration is from her latest book, *Roberto the Insect Architect,* which tells the story of a termite who dreams of designing and building houses. Laden constantly experiments with illustration techniques and credits a vivid imagination for her zany ideas. She lives in Seattle, Washington, where she's working hard on new books for children of all ages.

116
Artist: **Jeff Jackson**
Art Director: Neville Smith
Client: Statistics Canada
Medium: Chalk pastel on Arches paper
Size: 11" h x 11" w

117
Artist: **Dave McKean**
Art Director: Margaret Clark
Client: Pocket Books
Medium: Mixed, digital
Size: 14" h x 10" w

118
Artist: **Kent Williams**
Art Director: Dave McKean
Client: Allen Spiegel Fine Arts
Medium: Oil on canvas
Size: 26" h x 18" w

119
Artist: **Dave McKean**
Art Director: Margaret Clark
Client: Pocket Books
Medium: Mixed, digital
Size: 12" h x 16" w

116

117

118

120

Artist: **Jordin Isip**
Art Director: Herb Kohl
Client: The New Press
Medium: Mixed on paper
Size: 47" h x 30" w

121

Artist: **Laura Levine**
Art Director: Bob Kosturko
Client: Houghton Mifflin Company
Medium: Acrylic on masonite
Size: 22" h x 18" w

122

Artist: **Laura Levine**
Art Director: Bob Kosturko
Client: Houghton Mifflin Company
Medium: Acrylic on masonite
Size: 28" h x 24" w

123

Artist: **Laura Levine**
Art Director: Bob Kosturko
Client: Houghton Mifflin Company
Medium: Acrylic on masonite
Size: 36" h x 30" w

120

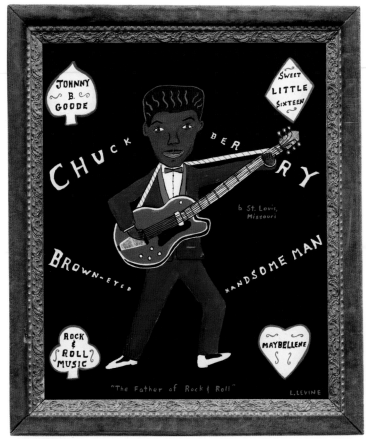

121

122

123

124
Artist: **Russ Wilson**
Art Directors: Chris Wood
                 Stephen Wirt
Client: Harcourt Brace & Company
Medium: Pastel on paper
Size: 18" h x 13" w

125
Artist: **Bruce Waldman**
Art Director: Martha Phillips
Client: The Franklin Library
Medium: Monoprint on Arches
Size: 26" h x 35" w

126
Artist: **Andrea Ventura**
Art Director: Gary Gifford
Client: Houghton Mifflin Company
          McDougal Littell
Medium: Mixed on paper
Size: 20" h x 16" w

127
Artist: **Andrea Ventura**
Art Director: Gary Gifford
Client: Houghton Mifflin Company
          McDougal Littell
Medium: Mixed on paper
Size: 20" h x 16" w

128
Artist: **Andrea Ventura**
Art Director: Gary Gifford
Client: Houghton Mifflin Company
          McDougal Littell
Medium: Mixed on paper
Size: 20" h x 16" w

124

125

126

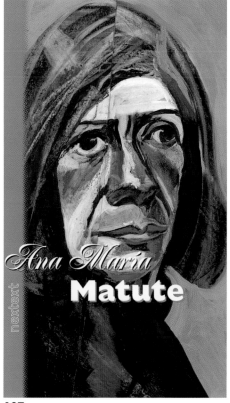

127

128

129
Artist: **Seymour Chwast**
Client: Walter Lorraine Books

130
Artist: **Balvis Rubess**
Art Director: Duncan Bock
Client: Rob Weisbach Books
Medium: Acrylic on board
Size: 11" h x 17" w

131
Artist: **Giselle Potter**
Art Director: Angela Carlino
Client: Atheneum Books for Young Readers
Medium: Gouache on paper

132
Artist: **Chris Sheban**
Art Director: Rita Marshall
Client: Creative Education
Medium: Watercolor, pencil on 90 lb.
　　　　Arches hot press paper
Size: 16" h x 9" w

133
Artist: **Edward Sorel**
Art Director: Ann Bobco
Client: Margaret McElderry Books
Medium: Pen & ink, watercolor on
　　　　mounted bond paper
Size: 20" h x 20" w

129

130

131

132

133

134
Artist: **John Thompson**
Art Director: Rita Marshall
Client: Creative Editions
Medium: Acrylic on Bristol board
Size: 13" h x 9" w

135
Artist: **James Ransome**
Art Director: Heather Wood
Client: Simon & Schuster Books for
    Young Readers
Medium: Acrylic on paper

136
Artist: **Wendell Minor**
Art Director: Al Cetta
Client: HarperCollins
Medium: Watercolor on cold press paper
Size: 10" h x 7" w

137
Artist: **John Thompson**
Art Director: Rita Marshall
Client: Creative Editions
Medium: Acrylic on Bristol board
Size: 13" h x 9" w

138
Artist: **James Ransome**
Art Director: Heather Wood
Client: Simon & Schuster Books for
    Young Readers
Medium: Acrylic on paper

134

135

136

137

138

139

Artist: **Marie Lessard**

Art Director: Monic Delorme

Client: Les Editions de la Courte Echelle

Medium: Monoprint, collage on paper

Size: 11" h x 8" w

140

Artist: **Maggie Taylor**

Art Director: Joni Friedman

Client: Berkley Books

Medium: Mixed on paper

Size: 11" h x 17" w

141

Artist: **Jeffrey Smith**

Art Directors: James McMullan
                Marjorie Palmer

Client: Reader's Digest

Medium: Watercolor on paper

Size: 10" h x 14" w

142

Artist: **Jonathon Rosen**

Client: Eleventh Hour Press

Medium: Digital

Size: 8" h x 11" w

139

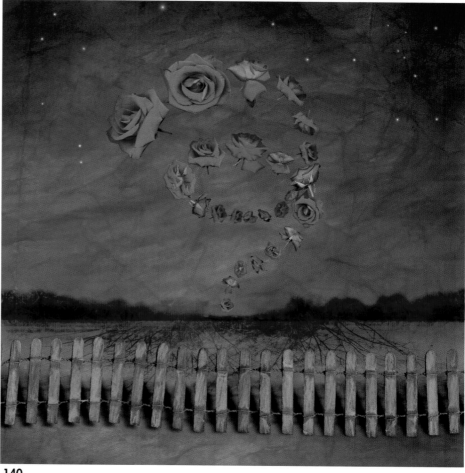

140

141

142

143
Artist: **Douglas Smith**
Art Director: Leslie Goldman
Client: Little, Brown & Company
Medium: Scratchboard, watercolor
Size: 15" h x 10" w

144
Artist: **Peter Sawchuk**
Art Director: Suzanne Joelson
Medium: Mixed, digital on paper
Size: 18" h x 42" w

145
Artist: **Geneviéve Côté**
Art Director: Diane Primeau
Client: Dominique & Friends Publishers
Medium: Mixed
Size: 7" h x 15" w

143

NEW YORK

The Voyage took nearly three weeks. Before his son's departure, Gregorii had pulled aside a middle-aged man and pleaded with him to look after his son during the trip. Bruno was a carpenter who had lost most of his family during the war. He was traveling alone and was happy to help this young man. Fortunately for Fedoshka, Bruno had brought more than enough food with him. Gregorii was led to believe that food would be provided, but that service only applied to first and second-class passengers, not to the steerage.

In steerage, the trip was long indeed. Bruno and Fedoshka would spend as much time on deck as possible. Down below the air was foul and the conditions cramped. Fedoshka soon learned from other passengers to layer up clothes and to keep all his valuables in his pockets. If his baggage was stolen, he at least would not lose everything.

There were only four stoves for the over 500 people in third class, so Fedoshka and his mentor usually ate cold meals. Their diet was comprised mainly of stale bread, hard-boiled eggs and sausage. Occasionally, they would heat up water and have tea. Fedoshka was often seasick, losing about ten pounds during the voyage.

It had been a foggy day and rumor was that they were along the American coast, but it was impossible to see much further than a couple hundred yards from the ship. Fedoshka and Bruno were sitting on deck, Bruno with his unlit pipe in his mouth.

146
Artist: **Eileen O'Connell**
Art Director: W. David Houser
Client: Creative Homeowner
Medium: Acrylic on board
Size: 12" h x 17" w

147
Artist: **Pascal Milelli**
Art Director: Katherine Campbell
Client: Wright Group Publishing
Medium: Oil on board
Size: 15" h x 13" w

148
Artist: **Leonid Gore**
Art Director: Ellen Friedman
Client: North-South Books
Medium: Acrylic on paper
Size: 12" h x 8" w

149
Artist: **Jerry Pinkney**
Art Director: Ellen Friedman
Client: Sea Star Books
Medium: Watercolor, pencil on paper
Size: 11" h x 9" w

150
Artists: **Mark Todd**
       Esther Watson
Art Director: Bob Kosturko
Client: Houghton Mifflin Company
Medium: Acrylic on paper
Size: 30" h x 24" w

146

147

148

149

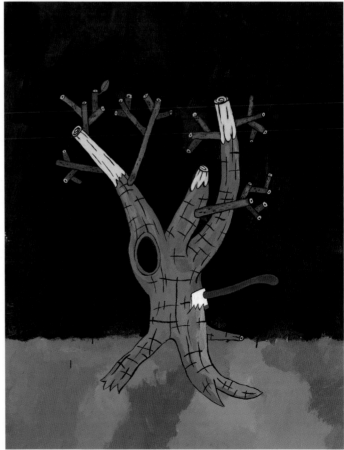

150

151

Artist: **Frances Jetter**

Art Director: Gerilee Hundt

Client: Chicago Review Press

Medium: Collage on paper

Size: 19" h x 14" w

152

Artist: **Mark Bischel**

Art Directors: Marshall Arisman
                Carl Titolo

Client: Self-published book

Medium: Silkscreen print on paper

Size: 14" h x 22" w

153

Artist: **John Collier**

Art Director: Vivian Ducas

Client: Harlequin Enterprises Ltd.

Medium: Pastel, watercolor on paper

Size: 13" h x 11" w

154

Artist: **Rob Wood**

Art Director: Carl Galian

Client: Ballantine Books

Medium: Acrylic on Strathmore board

Size: 14" h x 12" w

155

Artist: **Mark Bischel**

Art Directors: Marshall Arisman
                Carl Titolo

Client: Self-published book

Medium: Silkscreen print on paper

Size: 14" h x 22" w

151

152

153

154

155

156
Artist: **Melissa Sweet**
Art Director: Kristine Brogno
Client: Chronicle Books
Medium: Watercolor

157
Artist: **Susan Kathleen Hartung**
Art Director: Denise Cronin
Client: Viking Children's Books
Medium: Oil on paper

158
Artist: **C.F. Payne**
Art Director: David Gale
Client: Simon & Schuster Books
for Young Readers
Medium: Mixed on board

159
Artist: **C.F. Payne**
Art Director: David Gale
Client: Simon & Schuster Books
for Young Readers
Medium: Mixed on board

156

160

Artist: **Kadir Nelson**

Art Directors: Nancy Leo-Kelly
Atha Tehon

Client: Dial Books for Young Readers

Medium: Oil on paper

Size: 15" h x 10" w

161

Artist: **Jerry Pinkney**

Art Director: Atha Tehon

Client: Phyllis Fogelman Books

Medium: Watercolor, pencil on paper

Size: 11" h x 19" w

162

Artist: **Raúl Colón**

Art Director: Atha Tehon

Client: Dial Books for Young Readers

Medium: Watercolor, colored
pencil on paper

163

Artist: **Geneviève Côté**

Art Director: Diane Primeau

Client: Dominique & Friends

Medium: Mixed

Size: 11" h x 9" w

160

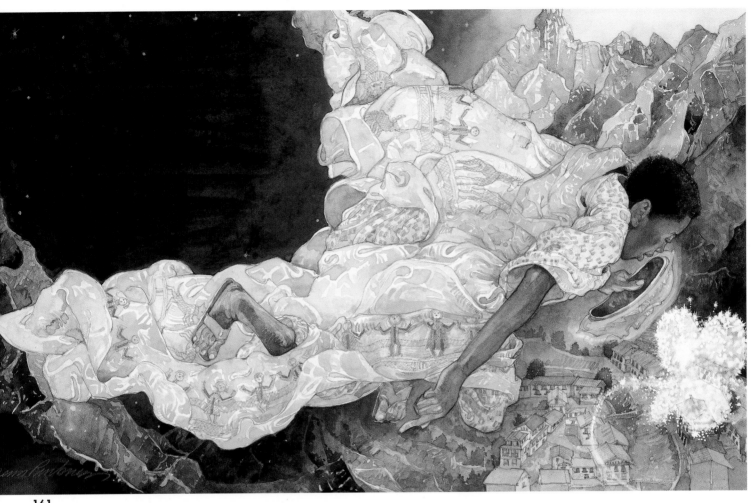

161

162

163

164
Artist: **Paul Meisel**
Art Director: Al Cetta
Client: HarperCollins
Medium: Alkyd on paper
Size: 12" h x 18" w

165
Artist: **Robert Crawford**
Art Director: Nick Krenitsky
Client: HarperCollins

166
Artist: **Hiroe Nakata**
Art Director: Sarah Reynolds
Client: Dutton Children's Books
Medium: Watercolor on paper
Size: 11" h x 21" w

167
Artist: **Hiroe Nakata**
Art Director: Sarah Reynolds
Client: Dutton Children's Books
Medium: Watercolor on paper
Size: 11" h x 21" w

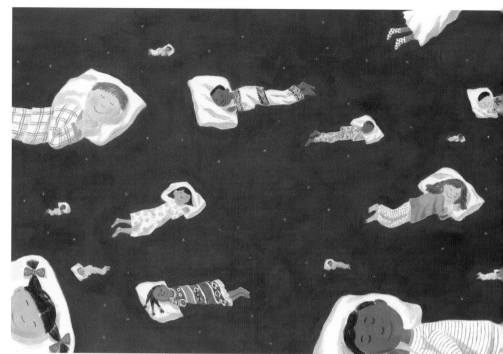

164

165

166

167

168
Artist: **Jeff Jackson**
Art Director: Neville Smith
Client: Statistics Canada
Medium: Chalk pastel on Arches paper
Size: 11" h x 11" w

169
Artists: **Steve Johnson**
      Lou Fancher
Art Director: Denise Cronin
Client: Viking Children's Books
Medium: Oil, string on paper

170
Artist: **Brett Helquist**
Art Director: Nick Krenitsky
Client: HarperCollins

171
Artist: **Peter de Sève**
Art Director: Roseanne Serra
Client: Penguin Putnam Inc.
Medium: Watercolor, ink on
      watercolor paper
Size: 15" h x 10" w

168

169

170

171

172
Artist: **Christian Clayton**
Art Directors: Paolo Pepe
　　　　　　Brigid Pearson
Client: Pocket Books/
　　　　Washington Square Press
Medium: Mixed
Size: 13" h x 9" w

173
Artist: **Lois Ehlert**
Art Director: Michael Farmer
Client: Harcourt Brace & Company
Medium: Collage, found objects
Size: 10" h x 20" w

174
Artist: **James Ransome**
Art Director: Martha Rago
Client: Henry Holt & Company
Medium: Oil on paper

172

173

174

175

Artist: **David Slonim**
Art Directors: Susan Pearson
Golda Laurens
Al Cetta
Client: HarperCollins
Medium: Oil on linen

176

Artist: **David Slonim**
Art Directors: Susan Pearson
Golda Laurens
Al Cetta
Client: HarperCollins
Medium: Oil on linen

177

Artist: **Loren Long**
Art Director: Nina Ignatowicz
Client: Henry Holt & Company
Medium: Acrylic on linen
Size: 16" h x 10" w

178

Artist: **Charlotte Noruzi**
Art Directors: Panio Gianopoulos
Susan Burns
Client: Bloomsbury USA
Medium: Collage
Size: 8" h x 5" w

179

Artist: **Jeffrey Fisher**
Art Director: Jennifer Heisley
Client: Viking/Penguin
Medium: Acrylic

175

176

177

178

179

180
Artist: **Yan Nascimbene**
Art Director: Jim Plumeri
Client: Bantam Doubleday Dell
Medium: Ink, watercolor on paper
Size: 18" h x 15" w

181
Artist: **Rafal Olbinski**
Art Director: Irene Gallo
Client: Tor Books
Medium: Acrylic on canvas

182
Artist: **Adam McCauley**
Art Directors: Madeline Budnick
Cynthia Wigginton
Client: Chronicle Books
Medium: Mixed on watercolor paper

183
Artist: **Adam McCauley**
Art Directors: Madeline Budnick
Cynthia Wigginton
Client: Chronicle Books
Medium: Mixed on watercolor paper

180

181

182

183

184
Artist: **William Steig**
Art Director: Alicia Mikles
Client: Joanna Cotler Books
Medium: Mixed on paper
Size: 8" h x 8" w

185
Artist: **Jerry Pinkney**
Art Director: Ellen Friedman
Client: Sea Star Books
Medium: Watercolor, pencil on paper
Size: 11" h x 9" w

186
Artist: **Patrick Arrasmith**
Art Director: Irene Gallo
Client: Tor Books
Medium: Scratchboard
Size: 15" h x 10" w

187
Artist: **Nobutsuna Watanabe**
Client: Hayakawa Publishing Corporation
Medium: Acrylic on paper
Size: 8" h x 6" w

188
Artist: **Betsy Lewin**
Art Director: Anahid Hamparian
Client: Simon & Schuster Books for
Young Readers
Medium: Watercolor on Strathmore Bristol
Size: 18" h x 24" w

184

185

186

187

188

189
Artist: **William Steig**
Art Director: Alicia Mikles
Client: Joanna Cotler Books
Medium: Mixed on paper
Size: 8" h x 8" w

190
Artist: **Andy Rash**
Art Director: David Saylor
Client: Arthur A. Levine Books
Medium: Gouache, ink on watercolor paper
Size: 10" h x 8" w

191
Artist: **G. Brian Karas**
Art Director: Alicia Mikles
Client: Joanna Cotler Books
Medium: Mixed on paper
Size: 12" h x 25" w

192
Artist: **David Shannon**
Art Director: Kathleen Westray
Client: Blue Sky Press
Medium: Acrylic on board
Size: 15" h x 22" w

193
Artist: **Charles Santore**
Art Directors: Cathy Goldsmith
                  Joanne Yates
Client: Random House Children's Publishing
Medium: Watercolor on Arches
           90 lb. paper

189

190

191

192

193

194
Artist: **Gary Baseman**
Art Director: Monte Beauchamp
Client: Blab
Medium: Acrylic on canvas
Size: 18" h x 18" w

195
Artist: **Greg Clarke**
Art Director: Ed Brash
Client: Callaway Editions

196
Artist: **Scott Nash**
Art Director: Anne Moore
Client: Candlewick Press
Medium: Watercolor
Size: 20" h x 32" w

197
Artist: **William Joyce**
Art Director: Alicia Mikles
Client: HarperCollins
Medium: Digital
Size: 10" h x 20" w

194

195

198

Artist: **Steven Guarnaccia**

Art Director: Susan Hochbaum

Client: Stewart, Tibori, & Chang

Medium: Digital

Size: 9" h x 7" w

199

Artist: **Steven Guarnaccia**

Art Director: Susan Hochbaum

Client: Stewart, Tibori, & Chang

Medium: Digital

Size: 9" h x 7" w

200

Artist: **Mark Matcho**

Art Director: Chip Kidd

Client: Black Book Illustration

Medium: Digital

Size: 11" h x 27" w

201

Artist: **Coco Masuda**

Art Director: Robbin Schiff

Client: Random House

Medium: Airbrush, colored pencil on paper

Size: 15" h x 12" w

202

Artist: **Greg Clarke**

Art Director: Gina Manola

Client: Galison Books

203

Artist: **Greg Clarke**

Art Director: Mary Schuck

Client: Crown Publishing

198

199

200

201

202

203

204
Artist: **Geneviève Côté**
Art Directors: Andree Lauzon
                Stephanie Jorisch
Client: Les 400 Coups Publishers
Medium: Mixed
Size: 11" h x 9" w

205
Artist: **Paul Cox**
Art Director: Roseanne Serra
Client: Penguin Putnam Inc.
Medium: Watercolor on paper

206
Artist: **Adam McCauley**
Art Director: Denise Cronin
Client: Viking Children's Books
Medium: Mixed on watercolor paper

207
Artist: **Derek Stukuls**
Size: 10" h x 8" w

204

205

206

207

208
Artist: **Ward Schumaker**
Art Directors: Carolyn Robertson
Jim Robertson
Client: The Yolly Bolly Press
Medium: Letterpress print

209
Artist: **Ward Schumaker**
Art Directors: Carolyn Robertson
Jim Robertson
Client: The Yolly Bolly Press
Medium: Letterpress print

210
Artist: **Mark Bischel**
Art Directors: Marshall Arisman
Carl Titolo
Client: Self-published book
Medium: Silkscreen print on paper
Size: 14" h x 22" w

211
Artist: **Ward Schumaker**
Art Directors: Carolyn Robertson
Jim Robertson
Client: The Yolly Bolly Press
Medium: Letterpress print

212
Artist: **Cathie Bleck**
Art Director: Ellen Ellchep
Client: Random House
Medium: Scratchboard, gouache, digital
on watercolor paper
Size: 17" h x 12" w

208

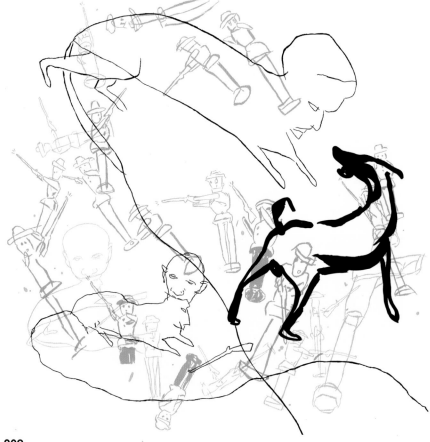

209

210

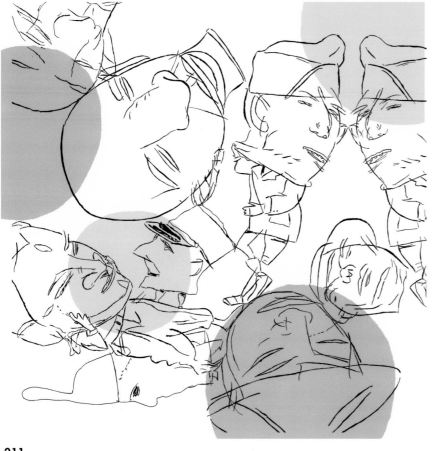

211

212

ADVERTISING

JURY

Peter Fiore, Chair
Illustrator

John Craig
Illustrator

Mary Kay DeLisle
Senior Art Director
Lyons Lavey Nickel Swift, Inc.

Dennis Dittrich
Illustrator

Joe Dizney
Design Director
The Wall Street Journal

Stephen T. Johnson
Illustrator

Loren Long
Illustrator

Mike Mrak
Design Director
Discover Magazine

Jean Tuttle
Illustrator

213 Gold Medal
Artist: **Jody Hewgill**
Art Directors: Scott Mires
Neill Archer Roan
Client: Arena Stage
Medium: Acrylic on gessoed board
Size: 14" h x 8" w

"This poster was commissioned by Arena Stage for their 2001 theatre season. 'Coyote Builds North America' is a play based on the Native American tale of Old Man Coyote, the ultimate trickster. Barry Lopez's poetic and imaginative script reveals Coyote in all his humanity. It was a delight to illustrate this character unabashedly displaying his vanity, foolishness, and primative appetites. This was my third season working with Arena Stage. The posters from my first season have been included in the permanent poster collection of The Library of Congress."

214 Gold Medal
Artist: **Bill Mayer**
Art Director: Harry Hartofelis
Client: Hartford Stage
Medium: Airbrush, gouache on
      hot press Strathmore
Size: 24" h x 18" w

Bill Mayer, a renowned illustrator of exceptional talent and infectious
good humor, is often imitated but rarely equaled. Mayer has won
dozens of awards from *Communication Arts, Graphis, Print,* the
Society of Illustrators, New York's Addy's, and Show South. Clients
such as Levi's for Women, José Quervo, *Time* magazine, IBM, Delta
Airlines, and RJR Nabisco reflect his unique ability to satisfy a varied
range of business sectors. Mayer's "Bright Eye's" stamps for the U.S.
Postal Service were one of the most collectible stamp series of the
decade, and the Tour de France posters he produced for Eric
Kessel/Kessel Kramer, Amsterdam, appeared on the cover of
Archive Magazine.

215 Silver Medal
Artist: **John H. Howard**
Art Director: Harriet Winner
Client: Booz-Allen & Hamilton
Medium: Acrylic on canvas
Size: 20" h x 84" w

"I love this boys' stuff: boats, trains, cars, and planes in a pristine landscape with no people to mess it up. With over a hundred listed ingredients from eco-systems to sputniks, I was a bit traumatized, but my first sketch had the same effect on my client, and the ensuing finish went through without any changes. Now, wow, a medal. I wish the rest of my life could be this smooth."

216 Silver Medal
Artist: **Martin Jarrie**
Art Director: Iris Brown
Client: Frederick Wildman and Sons
Medium: Acrylic on paper

Born in 1953 in the Vendee in France, the artist studied at the Ecole des Beaux-Arts d'Angers until 1978. He began his career as an illustrator in Paris, and in 1982 received his first prize, le Marker d'Argent. After six years of doing realistic advertising and editorial work, he changed styles, took on the pseudonym of Martin Jarrie, and began working with a new energy. In 1994 he had his first exhibition of personal works at the Galerie Michel Lagarde in Paris. His first children's book was *Toc Toc Monsieur Cric Crac,* and after a writer was inspired by some of his paintings, they collaborated on *le Colosse Machinal.* In 1997 he participated in the International Biennale d'Illustration at Bratislava, where he received two prizes.

217 Silver Medal
Artist: **Gary Kelley**
Art Directors: Scott Mires
Neill Archer Roan
Client: Arena Stage
Medium: Pastel on paper
Size: 22" h x 12" w

"With a client like Arena Stage, a Creative Director like Neill Archer Roan, and a story to tell like 'The Great White Hope,' there are no excuses."

218 Silver Medal
Artist: **Anita Kunz**
Art Director: Mark Seliger
Client: Rusty Truck
Medium: Mixed on board
Size: 15" h x 15" w

Born in Toronto in 1956, Anita Kunz graduated from the Ontario College of Art in 1978. Among her many international clients are *Time, Rolling Stone, Sports Illustrated, Newsweek, The Atlantic Monthly, The New Yorker, GQ, The New York Times,* Sony Music, Random House Publishing, and many others. Articles about her work have appeared in *Graphis, Communication Arts, Step-by-Step,* as well as many international publications. She has illustrated more than 50 book jackets. She is a lecturer, and teaches at the Illustration Academy in Kansas and Syracuse University. Kunz has won many prestigious awards and her work is held in permanent collections worldwide.

219
Artist: **Larry Moore**
Art Director: Scott Petit
Client: Fox Valley Blues Society
Medium: Pastel on paper
Size: 30" h x 12" w

220
Artist: **Gary Kelley**
Art Director: David Bartels
Client: Mississippi Delta Blues Festival
Medium: Pastel on paper
Size: 27" h x 16" w

221
Artist: **Douglas Fraser**
Art Director: Ken Giddon
Client: Rothman's Mens Clothing
Medium: Alkyd on canvas

222
Artist: **Larry Moore**
Art Director: Scott Sugiuchi
Client: Orlando Opera Company
Medium: Pastel on paper
Size: 20" h x 15" w

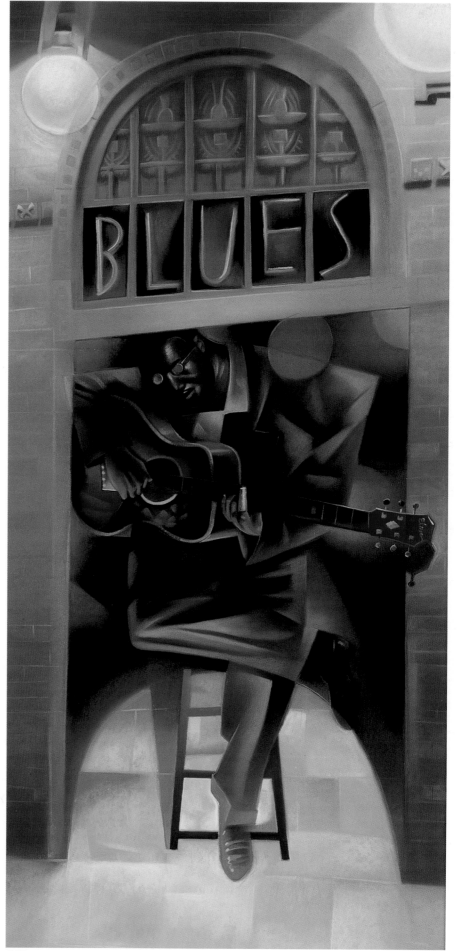

219

220

221

222

223

Artist: **Paul Rogers**

Art Director: Craig Denham

Client: University of Texas

Medium: Digital

Size: 14" h x 11" w

224

Artist: **Paul Rogers**

Art Director: Jamie Vernorsky

Client: Firestone Polymers

Medium: Digital

Size: 14" h x 11" w

225

Artist: **John Rush**

Art Director: Mitch Markovitz

Client: United States Steel

Medium: Oil on canvas

Size: 42" h x 28" w

226

Artist: **Murray Kimber**

Art Directors: Ken Jacobs
                Mary Starks

Client: Dover Pacific

Medium: Oil on canvas

Size: 20" h x 16" w

227

Artist: **Mark Summers**

Art Directors: Jean Croft
                Kent Joshpe

Client: Dupont

Medium: Scratchboard, watercolor

Size: 13" h x 11" w

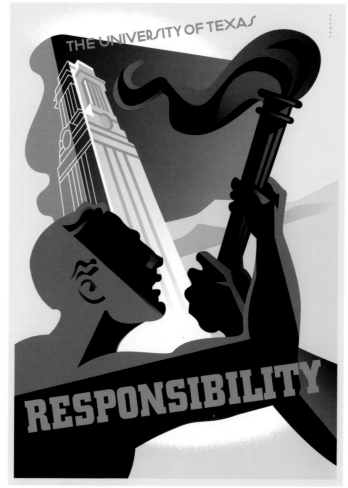

223

224

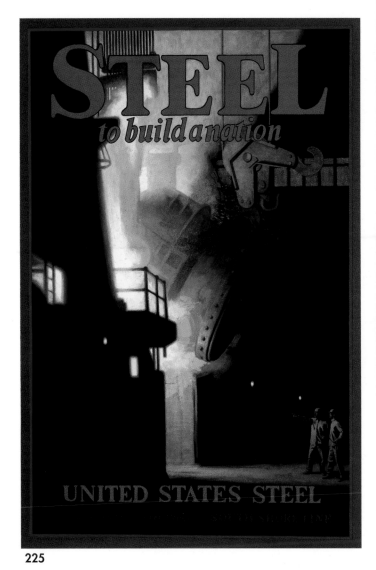

225

226

227

228
Artist: **Scott McKowen**
Client: Roundabout Theatre Company
Medium: Scratchboard

229
Artist: **Lisa French**
Art Director: Chris Chaffin
Client: See's Candies

230
Artist: **Scott McKowen**
Client: Roundabout Theatre Company
Medium: Scratchboard

231
Artist: **Mark Summers**
Art Directors: Clay Turner
Nancy Martin
Client: Trammell Crow Company
Medium: Scratchboard
Size: 13" h x 11" w

228

229

230

232

Artist: **Coco Masuda**
Art Director: Justine Tucker
Client: Target Corporation
Medium: Mixed on paper
Size: 12" h x 12" w

233

Artist: **Coco Masuda**
Art Director: Justine Tucker
Client: Target Corporation
Medium: Mixed on paper
Size: 12" h x 11" w

234

Artist: **Linda Fennimore**
Art Director: Chuck Slaughter
Client: Travel Smith
Medium: Colored pencil on paper
Size: 14" h x 11" w

235

Artist: **Linda Fennimore**
Art Director: Joanna Felder
Client: Travel Smith
Medium: Colored pencil on paper
Size: 13" h x 10" w

236

Artist: **Coco Masuda**
Art Director: Justine Tucker
Client: Target Corporation
Medium: Mixed on paper
Size: 12" h x 12" w

237

Artist: **Linda Fennimore**
Art Director: Linda Prosché
Client: Travel Smith
Medium: Colored pencil on paper
Size: 14" h x 10" w

232

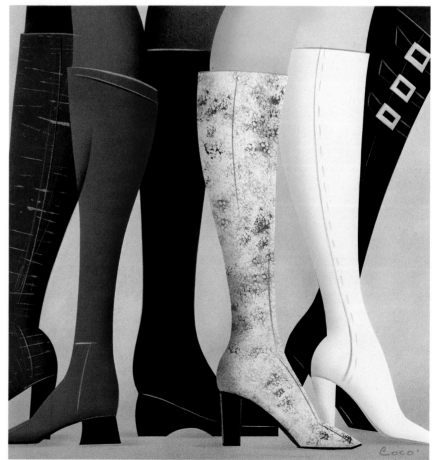

233

234

235

236

237

238
Artist: **Mark Todd**
Art Director: Kevin Brainard
Client: Jane Street Theatre
Medium: Digital

239
Artist: **Rowan Barnes-Murphy**
Art Director: Wendy Madeiras
Client: Macy's

240
Artist: **Jack Unruh**
Medium: Ink on board
Size: 20" h x 13" w

241
Artist: **Jessie Hartland**
Art Directors: Elizabeth Irwin
　　　　　　　Andy Gray
Client: Martha Stewart Living Magazine
Medium: Gouache on paper
Size: 17" h x 11" w

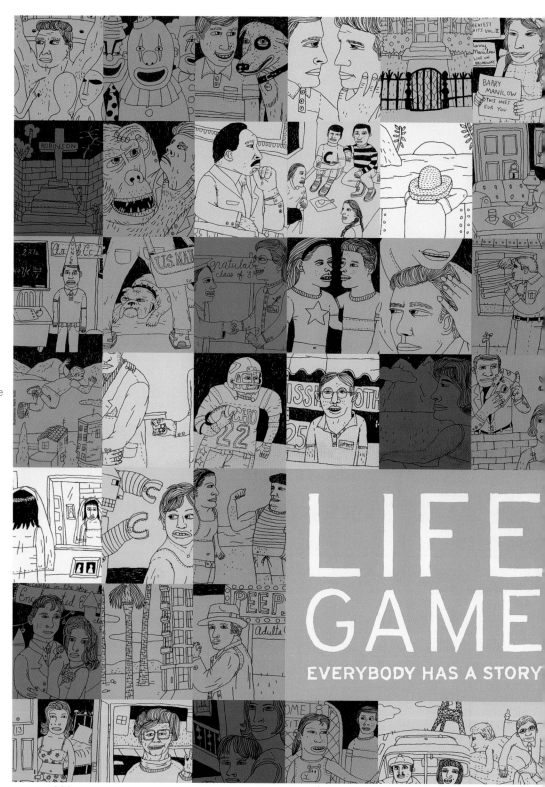

238

239

240

241

242
Artist: **Adam McCauley**
Art Director: Sandy Neill
Client: Vandoren Reeds
Medium: Mixed on watercolor paper

243
Artist: **Robert Neubecker**
Art Director: Julie Smith
Client: Citibank
Medium: Watercolor, ink on Arches
Size: 11" h x 8" w

244
Artist: **David Plunkert**
Art Director: Chad Bollenbach
Client: Madison Repertory Theatre
Medium: Mixed on paper
Size: 15" h x 10" w

245
Artist: **John Jay Cabuay**
Art Director: Laura Wills
Client: Screaming Mimi's
Medium: Digital (Illustrator 8.0)
Size: 11" h x 8" w

242

243

244

245

246
Artist: **David Plunkert**
Art Director: Chad Bollenbach
Client: Madison Repertory Theatre
Medium: Mixed on paper
Size: 15" h x 10" w

247
Artist: **Tim Bower**
Art Director: Erich Pfeifer
Client: ME VC

248
Artist: **John Cuneo**
Art Directors: Kit Hinrichs
                Karen Berndt
Client: University of Southern California
Medium: Pen & ink on Strathmore paper
Size: 11" h x 15" w

249
Artist: **Tim Bower**
Art Director: Erich Pfeifer
Client: ME VC

250
Artist: **Tim Bower**
Art Director: Erich Pfeifer
Client: ME VC

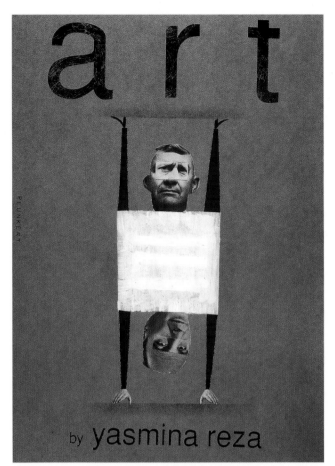

246

247

248

249

250

251
Artist: **Edel Rodriguez**
Art Director: Sandra Planeta
Client: Jujamcyn Theatre
Medium: Pastel, gouache, woodblock ink
　　　　on paper
Size: 39" h x 28" w

252
Artist: **James Bentley**
Art Director: Michel Wartelle
Client: Paradise Theatre
Medium: Mixed on board
Size: 10" h x 6" w

253
Artist: **David Beck**
Art Directors: Peter Robinson
　　　　　　 Bert Stern
Client: Cincinnati Playhouse in the Park
Medium: Mixed on Strathmore
　　　　cold press board
Size: 16" h x 13" w

254
Artist: **Scott Altmann**
Art Director: Michael Dubin
Client: Fadeaway Records
Medium: Oil on board
Size: 14" h x 30" w

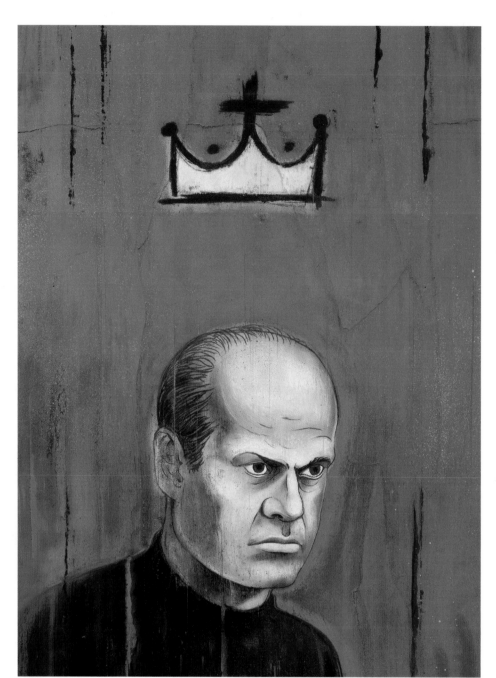

251

252

253

254

255
Artist: **Marco Ventura**
Art Director: Melanie Doherty
Client: St. Supery Wine
Medium: Mixed on masonite
Size: 4" h x 4" w

256
Artist: **Daniel Craig**
Art Director: Hilde McNeil
Client: Pioneer Theater Company
Medium: Acrylic on ragboard
Size: 18" h x 14" w

257
Artist: **David Bowers**
Art Director: Heather Cooley
Client: Millennium Import Company
Medium: Oil, cracking varnish on masonite
Size: 14" h x 4" w

258
Artist: **David Bowers**
Art Director: Heather Cooley
Client: Millennium Import Company
Medium: Oil, cracking varnish on masonite
Size: 14" h x 4" w

255

256

257

258

259
Artist: **Scott McKowen**
Client: Great Lakes Theater Festival
Medium: Scratchboard

260
Artist: **Albert Lorenz**
Client: Masterpieces
Medium: Pen & ink on Bristol board
Size: 24" h x 18" w

261
Artist: **Dan Cosgrove**
Art Director: Michael Guthrie
Client: International Paper
Medium: Digital
Size: 26" h x 21" w

262
Artists: **Steve Stroud**
　　　　 Daniel Dos Santos
Art Director: Clyde Goode
Client: General Electric
Medium: Oil on board
Size: 22" h x 32" w

259

260

261

262

263
Artist: **Ted Wright**
Art Director: Phil Montano
Client: Coors
Medium: Digital on canvas
Size: 30" h x 20" w

264
Artist: **Ted Wright**
Art Director: Tom Largess
Client: Montana Tourist Board
Medium: Digital on canvas
Size: 30" h x 20" w

265
Artist: **Ted Wright**
Art Director: Kathy Braun
Client: Bank of America
Medium: Digital on canvas
Size: 30" h x 20" w

263

264

265

266

Artist: **Loren Long**

Art Director: Peter Robinson

Client: Cincinnati Playhouse in the Park

Medium: Acrylic on linen

Size: 19" h x 11" w

267

Artist: **Rafal Olbinski**

Client: Warsaw Opera

Medium: Acrylic on canvas

Size: 36" h x 24" w

268

Artist: **Rafal Olbinski**

Client: Cincinnati Opera

Medium: Acrylic on canvas

Size: 30" h x 20" w

269

Artist: **Rafal Olbinski**

Art Director: Roxanne Moffitt

Client: Yale Repertory Theatre

Medium: Acrylic on canvas

Size: 30" h x 20" w

270

Artist: **Victor Gadino**

Art Director: Evey Korfias

Client: R.J. Reynolds

Medium: Oil on canvas

Size: 24" h x 30" w

266

267

268

269

270

271
Artist: **Rudy Gutierrez**
Client: Knitting Factory Records
Medium: Acrylic, oil crayon on board
Size: 31" h x 30" w

272
Artist: **Stephanie Henderson**
Art Director: Sue Kruchko
Client: Eric Miller Productions
Medium: Oil on canvas
Size: 22" h x 17" w

273
Artist: **Jody Hewgill**
Art Directors: Scott Mires
⠀⠀⠀⠀⠀⠀⠀⠀⠀Neill Archer Roan
Client: Arena Stage
Medium: Acrylic on gessoed board
Size: 18" h x 10" w

274
Artist: **Jody Hewgill**
Art Directors: Scott Mires
⠀⠀⠀⠀⠀⠀⠀⠀⠀Neill Archer Roan
Client: Arena Stage
Medium: Acrylic on gessoed board
Size: 16" h x 9" w

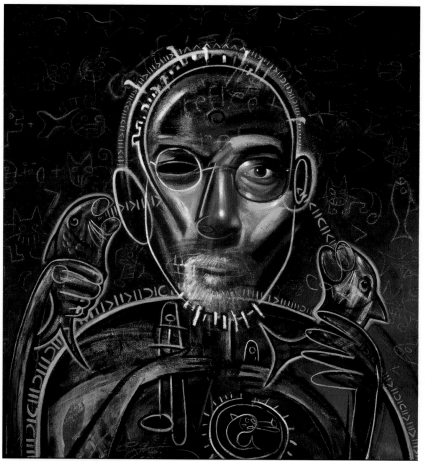

271

272

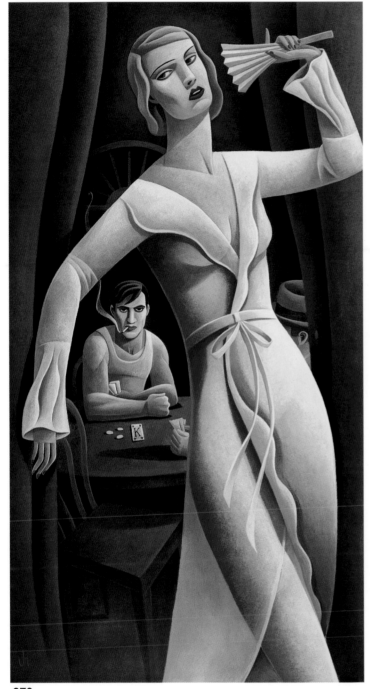

273

274

275
Artist: **Karen Santry**
Art Director: Sid Buck
Client: Dynasty Pools
Medium: Oil on canvas
Size: 21" h x 16" w

276
Artist: **Larry Moore**
Art Director: Scott Sugiuchi
Client: Orlando Opera Company
Medium: Pastel on paper
Size: 18" h x 15" w

277
Artist: **John Craig**
Art Director: Kit Hinrichs
Client: Organic

278
Artist: **Douglas Smith**
Art Director: Hilde McNeil
Client: Pioneer Theatre Company
Medium: Scratchboard, watercolor
Size: 11" h x 8" w

275

276

277

278

279
Artist: **Madeline von Foerster**
Client: The Long Black Veil (nightclub)
Medium: Acrylic on masonite
Size: 27" h x 24" w

280
Artist: **Bob Conge**
Art Director: Sue Kemp
Client: Oser Press
Medium: Pen & ink, watercolor on 140#
             Arches Roush watercolor paper
Size: 17" h x 14" w

281
Artist: **Gary Kelley**
Client: Theatre UNI (University of
             Northern Iowa)
Medium: Monotype on paper
Size: 14" h x 18" w

279

280

282

Artist: **David Lance Goines**

Client: Mr. Espresso

Medium: Offset lithography

Size: 24" h x 17" w

283

Artist: **Simon Shaw**

Art Director: Simon Cairns

Client: Burton Hollis Coffee

Medium: Mixed

Size: 7" h x 7" w

284

Artist: **Michael Schwab**

Art Directors: Dave Sanchez

           David Brown

Client: Gloria Ferrer

285

Artist: **John Thompson**

Art Director: Peter Perko

Client: Humber School for Writers

Medium: Acrylic on Bristol board

Size: 13" h x 9" w

282

283

284

285

286
Artist: **David Lance Goines**
Client: St. George Whiskey
Medium: Offset lithography
Size: 24" h x 17" w

287
Artist: **Marc Burckhardt**
Art Director: Jennifer Ward
Client: Spaten Brewing Company
Medium: Acrylic on wood
Size: 10" h x 10" w

288
Artist: **David Lance Goines**
Client: American Brass & Iron Foundry
Medium: Offset lithography
Size: 24" h x 17" w

289
Artist: **Rudy Gutierrez**
Client: Knitting Factory Records
Medium: Acrylic on board
Size: 12" h x 8" w

290
Artist: **Brad Yeo**
Art Directors: Patrick McCarthy
                Tomaso Milian
Client: Book of the Month Club
Medium: Acrylic on canvas
Size: 13" h x 25" w

286

287

288

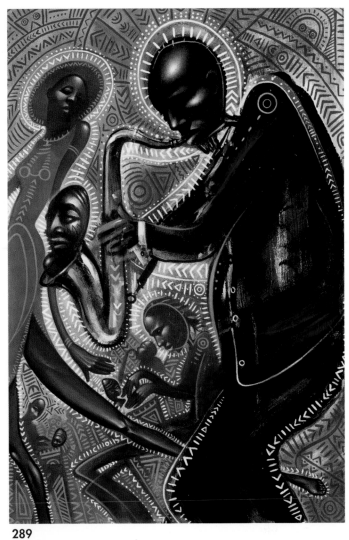

289

290

291
Artist: **Chris Gall**
Art Director: Margo Donaldson
Client: Indiana Farm Bureau
Medium: Alkyd on paper
Size: 16" h x 12" w

292
Artist: **John Patrick**
Art Directors: Kit Hinrichs
Brian Jacobs
Client: Edy's Grand Ice Cream
Medium: Gouache, watercolor,
acrylic on board
Size: 9" h x 25" w

293
Artist: **C.F. Payne**
Art Director: Kit Hinrichs
Client: Edy's Grand Ice Cream
Medium: Mixed on board
Size: 14' h x 25" w

291

292

293

294
Artist: **Leigh Wells**
Art Directors: Pam Williams
Rich Hollant
Client: Strathmore Paper Company
Medium: Mixed
Size: 23" h x 9" w

295
Artist: **Tom Christopher**
Art Director: Gary Reynolds
Client: Staples
Medium: Acrylic on canvas
Size: 48" h x 36" w

296
Artist: **Tom Christopher**
Art Director: Gary Reynolds
Client: Staples
Medium: Acrylic on canvas
Size: 48" h x 60" w

297
Artist: **Tom Christopher**
Art Director: Susan Simmons
Client: The New York Times

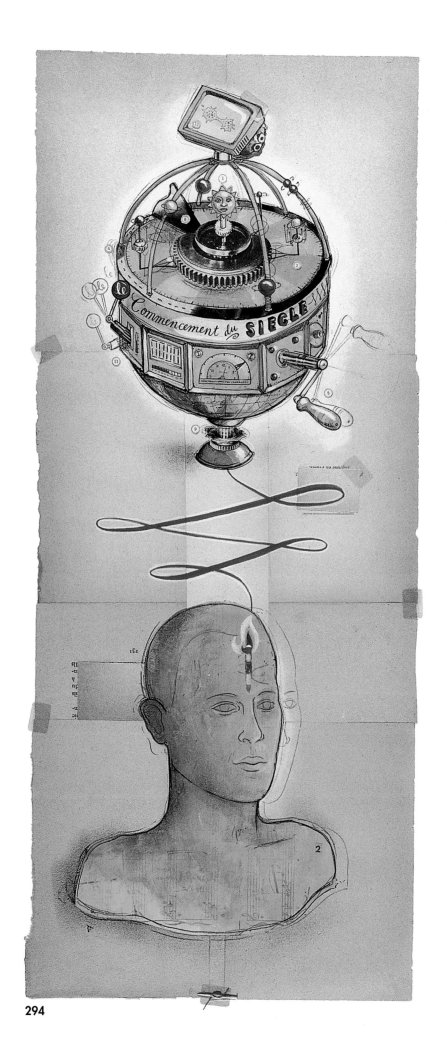

294

296

295

297

298
Artist: **N. Ascencios**
Ar Director: Julie Zerbo
Client: J. D'Addario & Co.

299
Artist: **Jean-Manuel Duvivier**
Art Director: Cesar Jachan
Client: Cannon Copiers France
Medium: Colored papers
Size: 27 cm h x 27 cm w

300
Artist: **Gary Baseman**
Art Director: Jeff Speiser
Client: Z-100 Radio
Medium: Acrylic on canvas
Size: 24" h x 18" w

301
Artist: **Mary GrandPré**
Art Director: Greer Sutter
Client: Lands' End
Medium: Pastel on paper
Size: 24" h x 18" w

298

299

300

301

302
Artist: **Pascal Milelli**
Art Director: Colin Vallance
Client: Kneipp Netherland BV
Medium: Oil on board
Size: 12" h x 6" w

303
Artist: **Chris Sheban**
Art Director: Al Shackelford
Client: Lands' End
Medium: Watercolor, pencil on 90 lb.
        Arches cold press paper
Size: 15" h x 12" w

304
Artist: **Bill Mayer**
Art Director: Branden Oldenburg
Client: Reel FX Creative Studios
Medium: Airbrush, gouache on
        hot press Strathmore

305
Artist: **Eriko Nagasawa**
Medium: Acrylic, gouache on board
Size: 57 cm h x 39 cm w

302

303

304

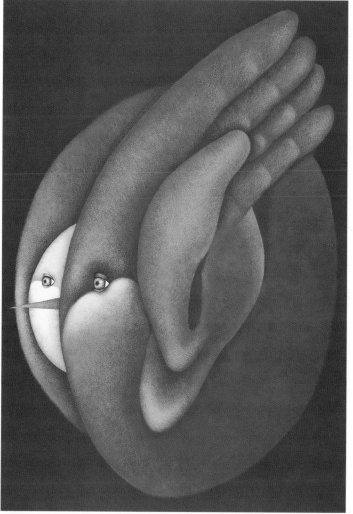

305

306
Artist: **Brad Holland**
Art Director: Mike Zban
Client: IDS Scheer
Medium: Acrylic on board

307
Artist: **Grgeory Manchess**
Art Director: Mort Kohn
Client: American Crystal Sugar
Medium: Oil on linen
Size: 21" h x 21" w

308
Artist: **Pascal Milelli**
Art Director: Ian Crawford
Client: Brew King
Medium: Oil on canvas
Size: 12" h x 29" w

309
Artist: **Wendell Minor**
Art Director: Bobette Wolf
Client: Adler Planetarium &
        Astronomy Museum
Medium: Acrylic on masonite
Size: 20" h x 22" w

306

307

308

309

INSTITUTIONAL

JURY

Peter Fiore, Chair
Illustrator

John Craig
Illustrator

Mary Kay DeLisle
Senior Art Director
Lyons Lavey Nickel Swift, Inc.

Dennis Dittrich
Illustrator

Joe Dizney
Design Director
The Wall Street Journal

Stephen T. Johnson
Illustrator

Loren Long
Illustrator

Mike Mrak
Design Director
Discover Magazine

Jean Tuttle
Illustrator

310 Gold Medal
Artist: **Istvan Orosz**
Art Director: Patricia Kowalczyk
Client: Marlena Agency/
Olver Dunlop Associates
Medium: Pen & ink

"This illustration was made for the cover of a calendar. In the calendar there are quotations by the contemporary Polish philosopher Leszek Kolakowski. He uses a lot of speculative paradoxes, so I wanted to use visual paradox describing concave and convex space. The Greek ruins relate to the origin of European philosophy, and the dead and the living tree refer to the resurrection of Platonic ideas. The style of the illustration is like the engravings of old encyclopedias and lexicons. I used this style because the viewer believes in this kind of old fashioned work, so it is easier 'to sell' a paradox or an 'impossible' thing in this way."

311 Gold Medal
Artist: **Noah Woods**
Art Directors: Tim Saver
               Ann Vorlicky
Client: Potlache
Medium: Mixed
Size: 16" h x 12" w

Noah Woods did this work for Kuester Partners in Minneapolis as a promotion for Potlache Papers. "It was the sketch I hoped they would choose. That doesn't always happen. I guess I'm batting .800." His media is collage paper, which for this work includes a book that's 80 years old, junk mail, and even his laundry list. "My studio isn't filled with paper, though. It's funny, it flows in and right out."

312 Silver Medal
Artist: **John Jude Palencar**
Art Director: Arnold Fenner
Client: Spectrum Design
Medium: Oil on sealed ragboard
Size: 30" h x 37" w

Artist and illustrator John Jude Palencar has collected more than 200 honors, including Gold and Silver medals from the Society of Illustrators, two Gold Book Awards from Spectrum, and two Best Paperback Cover Awards from the Association of Science Fiction and Fantasy Artists. His work has appeared on hundreds of covers for authors such as H.P. Lovecraft, Ursula LeGuin, Marion Zimmer Bradley, Octavia Butler, and Stephen King, as well as assignments for *Smithsonian* and *National Geographic*. Palencar has been a featured artist in *Idea* magazine, Japan. He was an Artist in Residence in Ireland where he was included in the exhibition, "Images of Ireland," at the National Museum in Dublin.

313
Artist: **Gary Kelley**
Art Directors: Talitha Harper
Mike Hammer
Client: Step-By-Step Graphics
Medium: Pastel on paper
Size: 22" h x 14" w

314
Artist: **Linda Montgomery**
Art Director: Andy Dearwater
Client: Hermann Hospital/Healing
Magazine
Medium: Mixed on paper
Size: 16" h x 12" w

313

314

315
Artist: **Gary Kelley**
Art Director: Jim Burke
Client: Dellas Graphics
Medium: Pastel on paper
Size: 24" h x 17" w

316
Artist: **Jack Unruh**
Art Director: Steve Frykholm
Client: Herman Miller
Medium: Ink, watercolor on board
Size: 17" h x 25" w

317
Artist: **David Hollenbach**
Art Director: Steve Gabor
Client: Salvato, Coe & Gabor Associates
Medium: Mixed on paper
Size: 11" h x 11" w

315

316

317

318
Artist: **Chris Gall**
Client: Simuflite Inc.
Medium: Alkyd on paper
Size: 12" h x 18" w

319
Artist: **Tom Christopher**
Art Director: Peter Schaefer
Client: The New York Times
Medium: Acrylic on canvas
Size: 48" h x 33" w

320
Artist: **David Lance Goines**
Client: University of California, Berkeley
Medium: Offset lithography
Size: 24" h x 16" w

321
Artist: **Vicki Wehrman**
Art Director: Richard Wehrman
Client: The Heartwork Institute
Medium: Digital
Size: 11" h x 8" w

322
Artist: **Yan Nascimbene**
Art Director: Laura Rioux
Client: University of California
     Botanical Garden
Medium: Ink, watercolor on paper

318

319

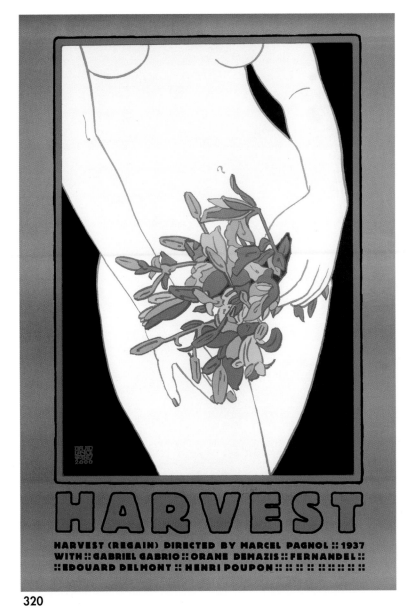

320

321

322

323
Artist: **Jim Burke**
Client: Dellas Graphics
Medium: Oil on board
Size: 20" h x 15" w

324
Artist: **Josh George**
Art Director: Clint & Ann Marie Jayne
Client: Jayne Gallery
Medium: Mixed on board
Size: 24" h x 30" w

325
Artist: **Michael Deas**
Art Director: Carl Herrman
Client: U.S. Postal Service
Medium: Oil

323

324

325

326
Artist: **Mike Benny**
Art Director: Bob Beyn
Client: Seraphein Beyn
Medium: Acrylic
Size: 20" h x 28" w

327
Artist: **David Uhl**
Client: Harley Davidson
Medium: Watercolor on clayboard
Size: 24" h x 18" w

328
Artist: **David Uhl**
Client: Harley Davidson
Medium: Gouache on clayboard
Size: 16" h x 20" w

329
Artist: **David Uhl**
Client: Harley Davidson
Medium: Gouache on clayboard
Size: 16" h x 20" w

326

327

328

329

330
Artist: **Raymond Olivere**
Art Director: Grey Hirschfeld
Medium: Oil on canvas
Size: 30" h x 20" w

331
Artist: **Grgeory Manchess**
Client: American Cancer Society
Medium: Oil on linen
Size: 26" h x 20" w

330

332
Artist: **Wilson McLean**
Art Director: Rex Peteet
Medium: Oil on canvas

333
Artist: **Albert Lorenz**
Client: Masterpieces
Medium: Mixed on Bristol board

334
Artist: **Bruce Waldman**
Art Directors: Sharon Shiraga
                          Alysia Duckler
Client: Alysia Duckler Gallery
Medium: Monoprint on Reves-BFA
Size: 24" h x 32" w

332

333

334

335
Artist: **Teresa Fasolino**
Art Director: Audrey Shacknow
Client: The Newborn Group
Medium: Oil on canvas
Size: 14" h x 11" w

336
Artist: **Wilson McLean**
Art Director: Rex Peteet
Medium: Oil on canvas

335

337
Artist: **Robert Giusti**
Art Director: Joan Sigman
Client: The Newborn Group
Medium: Acrylic on canvas board
Size: 14" h x 11" w

338
Artist: **Lorena Pugh**
Medium: Oil on linen
Size: 12" h x 40" w

339
Artist: **Jack Unruh**
Art Director: Scott Ray
Client: Dallas Society of Visual
        Communications
Medium: Ink, watercolor on board
Size: 30" h x 28" w

337

338

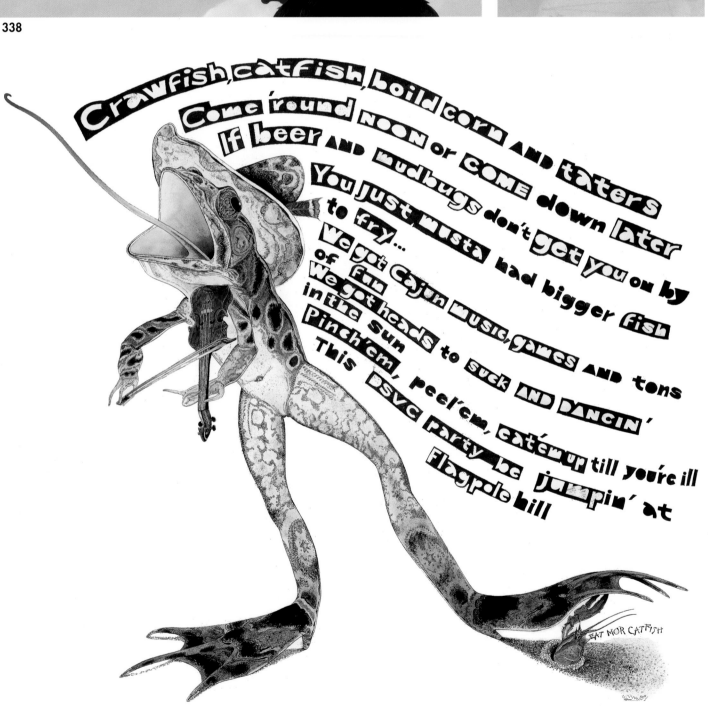

339

340
Artist: **George Schill**
Art Director: Patty Flauto
Client: American Greetings
Medium: Acrylic
Size: 10" h x 8" w

341
Artist: **Gary Baseman**
Client: Best Foundation
Medium: Acrylic on canvas
Size: 12" h x 12" w

342
Artist: **Gary Baseman**
Client: Society of Illustrators Los Angeles
Medium: Acrylic on canvas
Size: 24" h x 18" w

340

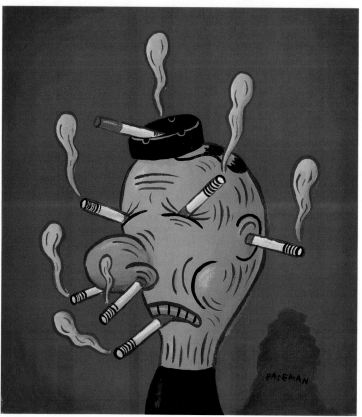

341

343
Artist: **Chris Gall**
Art Director: Mark Murphy
Client: Murphy Design
Medium: Scratchboard, digital on paper
Size: 14" h x 14" w

344
Artist: **Gary Locke**
Art Director: Ralph Kaufer
Client: Core America
Medium: Watercolor, colored pencil,
        airbrush on watercolor board
Size: 12" h x 12" w

345
Artist: **Chris Gall**
Art Director: Susan Manion
Client: Father's Day Council of Tucson
Medium: Scratchboard, digital on paper
Size: 14" h x 14" w

343

344

346
Artist: **Paul Davis**
Art Directors: Kit Hinrichs
Leslie Stitzlein
Client: Tenfold
Medium: Acrylic

347
Artist: **Peter de Sève**
Art Director: Joe Ciardiello
Client: Society of Illustrators
Medium: Watercolor, ink on
watercolor paper
Size: 11" h x 8" w

348
Artist: **Paul Cox**
Art Director: Jeremy Kaplan
Client: Madison Square Garden
Medium: Watercolor on paper
Size: 11" h x 13" w

346

347

349
Artist: **Joe Sorren**
Art Director: Mark Murphy
Client: Fortran Printing
Medium: Acrylic on canvas

350
Artist: **Joe Sorren**
Client: Heritage Square/Vanlandingham
    Cattle
Medium: Acrylic on canvas

351
Artist: **Bill Mayer**
Art Director: Jim Burke
Client: Dellas Graphics
Medium: Airbrush, gouache on
    hot press Strathmore

352
Artist: **Joe Sorren**
Art Director: Jim Burke
Client: Dellas Graphics
Medium: Acrylic on canvas

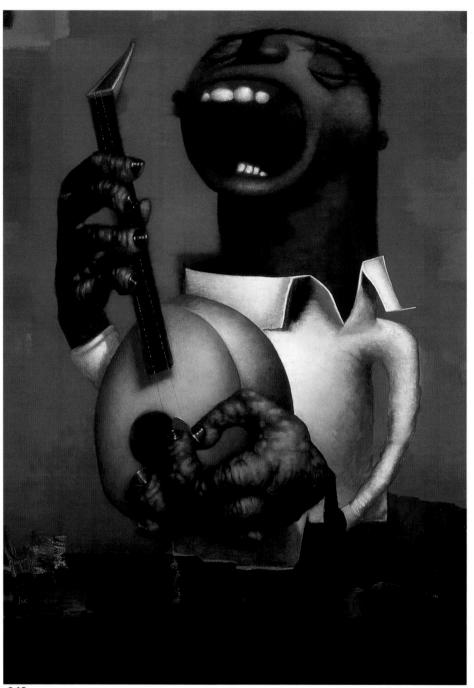

349

350

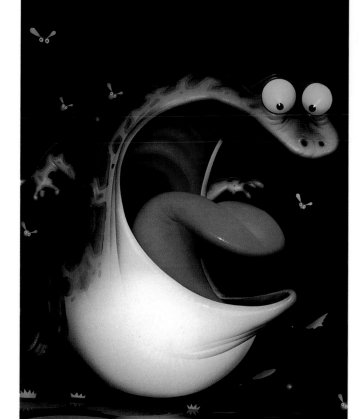

351

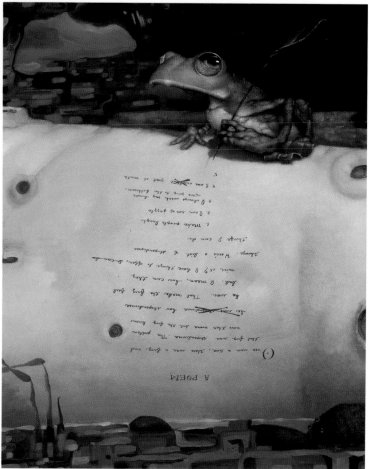

352

353
Artist: **Raúl Colón**
Art Director: Hilde McNeil
Client: Arizona Theatre
Medium: Watercolor, colored pencil
        on paper
Size: 13" h x 11" w

354
Artist: **Loren Long**
Art Director: Jim Burke
Client: Dellas Graphics
Medium: Acrylic on linen
Size: 18" h x 14" w

355
Artist: **Loren Long**
Art Director: Shannon Werling
Client: Cincinnati Chamber of Commerce
Medium: Acrylic on board
Size: 18" h x 14" w

356
Artist: **Mark Summers**
Art Director: Steve Krupsky
Client: Hasbro
Medium: Scratchboard, watercolor
Size: 17" h x 17" w

353

354

355

356

357
Artist: **Lee Ballard**
Art Director: Doug Cunningham
Client: Impact Gallery
Medium: Oil on linen
Size: 46" h x 24" w

358
Artist: **Donato**
Art Director: Toby Schwartz
Client: Doubleday Direct
Medium: Oil on paper on masonite
Size: 37" h x 30" w

359
Artist: **Phil Boatwright**
Client: Ussery Printing
Medium: Mixed on Strathmore board
Size: 14" h x 7" w

360
Artist: **Michael Gibbs**
Art Director: Roy Comiskey
Client: American Society for
        Industrial Security
Medium: Acrylic, digital on watercolor paper
Size: 16" h x 12" w

357

358

360

359

361

Artist: **Sally Wern Comport**

Art Director: Laurel S. Rummel

Client: Habitat for Humanity International

Medium: Mixed on coquille board

Size: 15" h x 13" w

362

Artist: **Bill Cigliano**

Art Director: Shaul Tsemach

Client: Johns Hopkins University

Medium: Oil, varnish on gessoed board

Size: 16" h x 12" w

363

Artist: **C.F. Payne**

Art Directors: Kit Hinrichs
                 Karen Berndt

Client: University of Southern California
          Office of Admissions

Medium: Mixed on board

Size: 15" h x 11" w

361

362

364
Artist: **Stephen T. Johnson**
Client: Manpower, Inc.

365
Artist: **William Hood**
Art Director: Mark Gormley
Client: Salvato, Coe & Gabor Associates
Medium: Acrylic on paper
Size: 12" h x 12" w

366
Artist: **Mark Summers**
Art Director: Sui Mon Wu
Client: Barnes & Noble
Medium: Scratchboard

367
Artist: **Brad Holland**
Client: Center for the Book Arts, NYC
Medium: Ink on paper

368
Artist: **Brad Holland**
Art Director: Dan Dyksen
Client: The Illustration Conference/
American Showcase
Medium: Pastel on paper

364

365

366

367

"THAT'S NOT ART THAT'S ILLUSTRATION"
Everybody is an artist these days. Rock and Roll singers are artists. So are movie directors, performance artists, make-up artists, tattoo artists, con artists and rap artists. Madonna is an artist because she explores her own sexuality. Snoop Doggy Dogg is an artist because he explores other peoples sexuality. Victims who express their pain are artists. So are guys in prison who express themselves on shirt cardboard. Even consumers are artists when they express themselves in their selection of commodities. The only people left who seem not to be artists are illustrators.

HOLLAND

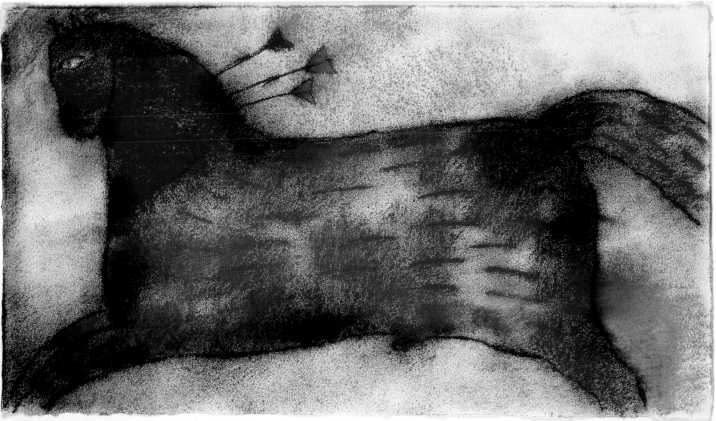

368

369
Artist: **Jean-Manuel Duvivier**
Art Director: Bob Verschuren
Client: Electrabel
Medium: Colored papers
Size: 27 cm h x 27 cm w

370
Artist: **Kris Hargis**
Art Director: Joe Cachero
Client: Starbucks Coffee
Medium: Acrylic, collage, pencil on panel
Size: 17" h x 11" w

371
Artist: **Kris Hargis**
Art Director: Joe Cachero
Client: Starbucks Coffee
Medium: Acrylic, collage, pencil on panel
Size: 17" h x 11" w

372
Artist: **Linda Helton**
Art Director: Art Garcia
Client: Texas Natural Resources
          Conservation Council
Medium: Acrylic on paper
Size: 17" h x 36" w

369

370

371

372

373
Artist: **John Collier**
Art Director: Mark Greer
Client: Domtar Inc. Paper Manufacturer
Medium: Monoprint
Size: 13" h x 13" w

374
Artist: **David Lesh**
Art Director: Clint Morgan
Client: ACE
Medium: Mixed on Strathmore
Size: 10" h x 8" w

375
Artist: **Paul Davis**
Client: School of Visual Arts

376
Artist: **Jim Frazier**
Art Director: Philip Taciak
Client: Sylvan Learning Systems Inc.

377
Artist: **George Schill**
Art Director: Patty Flauto
Client: American Greetings
Medium: Acrylic
Size: 10" h x 8" w

373

374

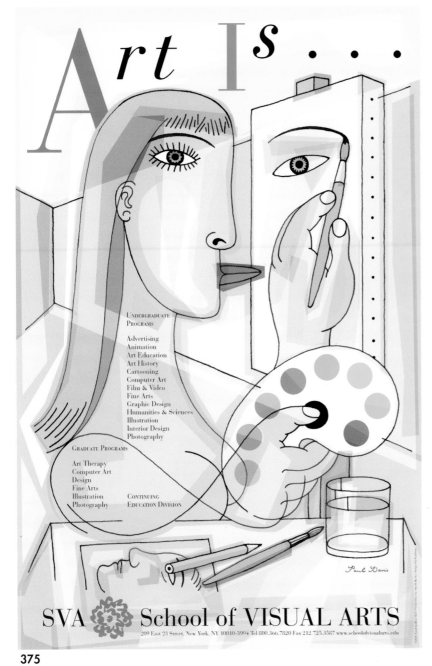

375

376

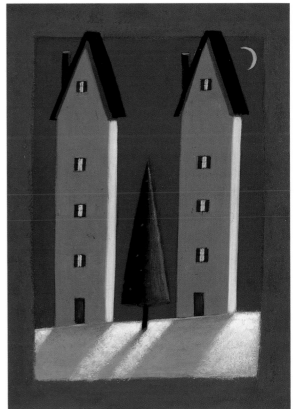

377

378
Artist: **Maria Carluccio**
Art Director: Julie McFarland
Client: Hallmark Cards, Inc.
Medium: Collage
Size: 6" h x 7" w

379
Artist: **Juliette Borda**
Art Director: Scott Lambert
Client: Fraser Papers
Medium: Gouache on paper
Size: 10" h x 8" w

380
Artist: **Craig Frazier**
Art Director: Conrad Jorgensen
Client: GATX Capital
Medium: Digital
Size: 23" h x 16" w

381
Artist: **Craig Frazier**
Art Director: Gordon Mortensen
Client: Bright Star
Medium: Digital
Size: 23" h x 19" w

382
Artist: **Craig Frazier**
Art Director: Tony Catlin
Client: Forrester Research, Inc.
Medium: Digital
Size: 23" h x 19" w

378

379

381

382

383
Artist: **David Wilcox**
Art Directors: Kit Hinrichs
Leslie Stitzlein
Client: Tenfold Corporation
Medium: Vinyl acrylic on hardboard
Size: 15" h x 20" w

384
Artist: **Wilson McLean**
Client: The Newborn Group
Medium: Oil on canvas

385
Artist: **Murray Kimber**
Art Director: Susan Skarsgard
Client: General Motors
Medium: Oil on canvas
Size: 20" h x 16" w

386
Artist: **John H. Howard**
Art Director: Joan Sigman
Client: The Newborn Group
Medium: Acrylic on paper

387
Artist: **Sally Wern Comport**
Art Director: Matt Marsh
Client: National Labor Federation
Medium: Mixed on coquille board
Size: 11" h x 15" w

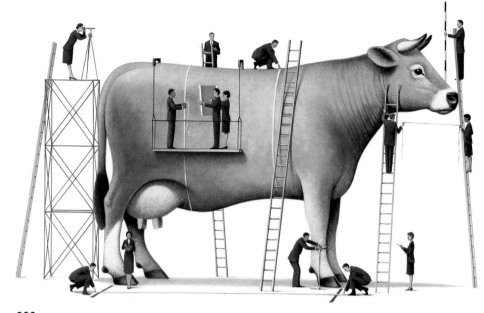

383

384

385

386

387

388
Artist: **John H. Howard**
Client: The National Labor Federation
Medium: Acrylic on canvas
Size: 33" h x 26" w

389
Artist: **John H. Howard**
Art Director: Joan Sigman
Client: The Newborn Group
Medium: Acrylic on canvas
Size: 36" h x 48" w

390
Artist: **Mark Ulriksen**
Art Director: Oddo de Grandis
Client: Galleria Communale d'Arte
            Moderna e Contemporanea
Medium: Tempera on board

388

389

390

391
Artist: **Roberto Parada**
Art Director: Matt Marsh
Client: Bay Area Alternative Press
Medium: Oil on canvas
Size: 20" h x 16" w

392
Artist: **Josef Gast**
Art Director: Steve Gabor
Client: Salvato, Coe & Gabor Associates
Medium: Gouache on Typak
Size: 11" h x 11" w

393
Artist: **Loren Long**
Art Directors: Doug Hardenburgh
Lisa Simacre
Client: Stackwoods Restaurant/
Nebraska Smokehouse
Medium: Oil
Size: 26" h x 89" w

394
Artist: **Raymond Verdaguer**
Art Director: Susan Skarsgard
Client: General Motors
Medium: Multi-colored linoleum cut on paper
Size: 16" h x 12" w

395
Artist: **Elvis Swift**
Art Director: Julie Mellen
Client: Fraser Papers
Medium: Ink on bond paper
Size: 5" h x 4" w

391

392

393

394

395

UNCOMMISSIONED/
UNPUBLISHED

JURY

Tim O'Brien, Chair
Illustrator

Gary Baseman
Illustrator

Mary Lynn Blasutta
Illustrator

Kelly Doe
Art Director
The Washington Post

Geraldine Hessler
Entertainment Weekly

Robert Neubecker
Illustrator

John Jude Palencar
Illustrator

David Saylor
VP/Creative Director, Book
Group, Scholastic Press

Mark Summers
Illustrator

396 Gold Medal
Artist: **John Collier**
Medium: Monoprint
Size: 12" h x 8" w

This work is a digitally enhanced monoprint. The subject is the rapper Rakim whose face Collier felt lent itself to black and white. He sought the texture of an old Polaroid negative, subtle but dense.

397 Silver Medal
Artist: **Etienne Delessert**
Medium: Watercolor
Size: 7" h x 5" w

The fifty works for "Birds of Prey" were completed by Etienne Delessert in a scant three months. They were shown last August in the 11th century castle Aven-chay in Switzerland. Delessert has shown the birds in transition as they become people, as we are ourselves at some time birds of prey.

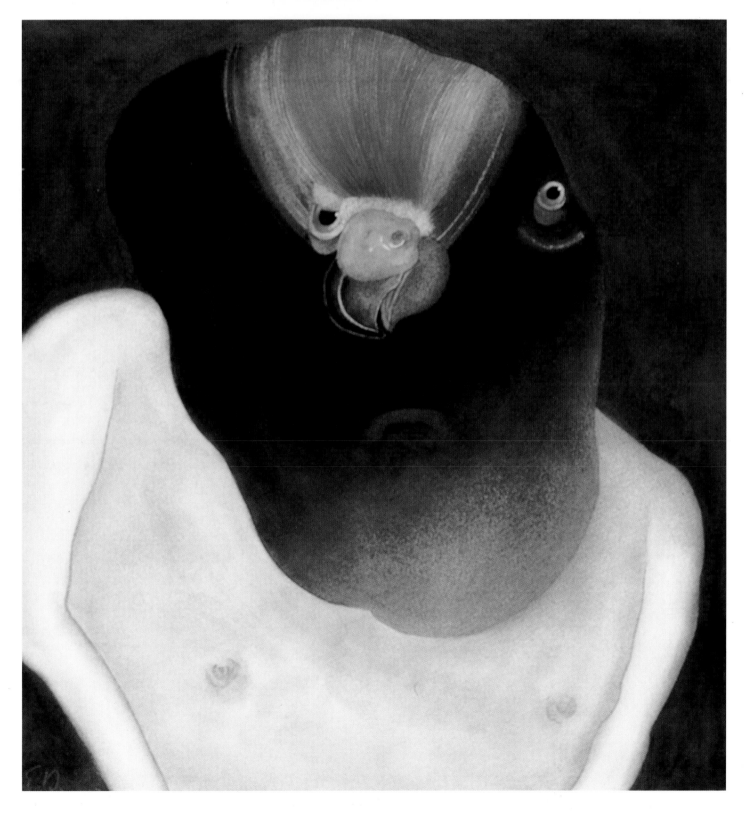

398 Silver Medal
Artist: **Lisa French**
Medium: Oil on board
Size: 19" h x 13" w

"Although this winning piece is typically invented realism, it is different than most of my commissioned projects in mood, coloration, and media. Since I have been both freelancing and teaching illustration in recent years, it has been a rare thing to find the time for self-initiated projects like this. And so it was an inspired work and a very satisfying personal experience, all the more encouraging because it has received this recognition by my professional peers and associates. In this time of digital dominance within the field of graphic arts, I suppose I have exposed my loyalty to more traditional art forms. I certainly hope that some art directors share this nostalgic inclination and see some possible application for such imagery."

399 Silver Medal
Artist: **Gary Taxali**
Medium: Alkyd on masonite
Size: 24" h x 32" w

"Packaging illustration really interests me; much of it can be pretty awe inspiring to the point of high art. This painting, 'America Lucky Service,' is one from a series of pictures which is a homage of sorts to the art of Japanese packaging. In particular, this work focuses on images of candy, toy, and book packaging. I began by creating a series of fictional products and characters; even the fonts (though accurate in some cases) are pretty much bastardized. The character in this painting is a chocolate candy egg man. I imagine a recurring character that spins off into a Saturday morning cartoon, merchandise galore, and perhaps even a spokesperson for a political party. Ah yes, commercial exploitation at its finest."

400
Artist: **Etienne Delessert**
Medium: Watercolor

401
Artist: **Etienne Delessert**
Medium: Watercolor

402
Artist: **Brad Holland**
Medium: Acrylic on board

403
Artist: **Peter Ambush**
Medium: Ink, oil

404
Artist: **Jonathan Weiner**
Medium: Oil on board
Size: 18" h x 20" w

400

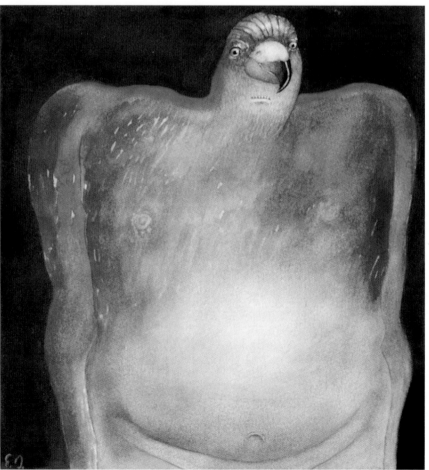

401

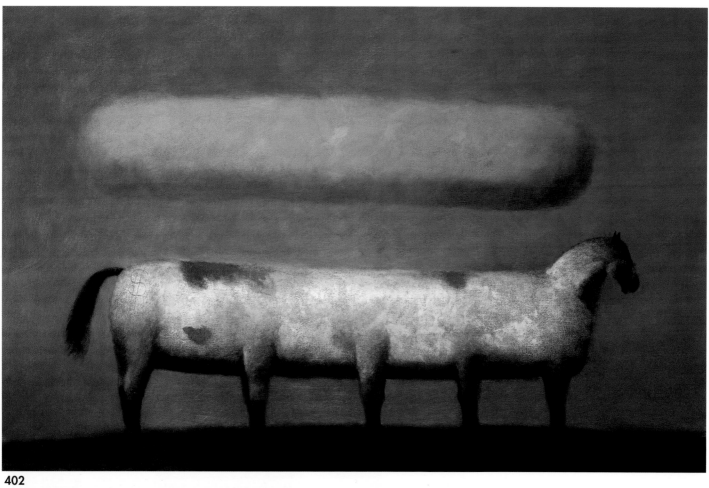

402

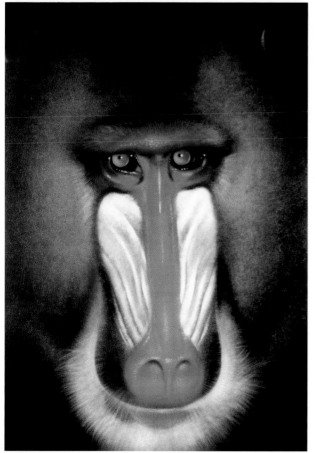

403

404

405
Artist: **Jonathan Weiner**
Medium: Oil on board
Size: 30" h x 20" w

406
Artist: **Joe Sorren**
Medium: Acrylic on canvas
Size: 52" h x 44" w

407
Artist: **Gabe Leonard**
Medium: Acrylic, colored pencil
Size: 21" h x 17" w

408
Artist: **Joe Sorren**
Medium: Acrylic on canvas
Size: 36" h x 24" w

409
Artist: **Malcolm Tarlofsky**

405

406

407

408

409

410
Artist: **Brad Holland**
Medium: Acrylic on board

411
Artist: **Jody Hewgill**
Medium: Acrylic on gessoed board
Size: 12" h x 10" w

412
Artist: **Phung Huynh**
Medium: Mixed, oil on canvas
Size: 53" h x 35" w

413
Artist: **Jim Frazier**

414
Artist: **Jason Nobriga**
Medium: Oil on canvas
Size: 48" h x 36" w

410

411

412

413

414

415
Artist: **Etienne Delessert**
Medium: Watercolor

416
Artist: **Eric Bowman**
Medium: Oil on masonite
Size: 17" h x 14" w

417
Artist: **Douglas Jones**
Medium: Watercolor, gouache on paper
Size: 10" h x 8" w

418
Artist: **Eric Bowman**
Medium: Oil on board
Size: 18" h x 14" w

415

416

417

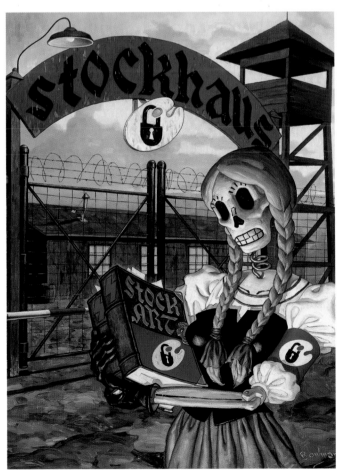

418

419
Artist: **Tifenn Python**
Medium: Mixed on paper
Size: 18" h x 16" w

420
Artist: **Josue R. Evilla**
Medium: Watercolor, gouache on Somerset
Size: 7" h x 6" w

421
Artist: **Merritt Dekle**
Medium: Acrylic
Size: 12" h x 8" w

422
Artist: **Regan Todd Dunnick**
Medium: Acrylic on cardboard
Size: 16" h x 12"

423
Artist: **Lynn Bennett**
Medium: Collage on paper
Size: 14" h x 10" w

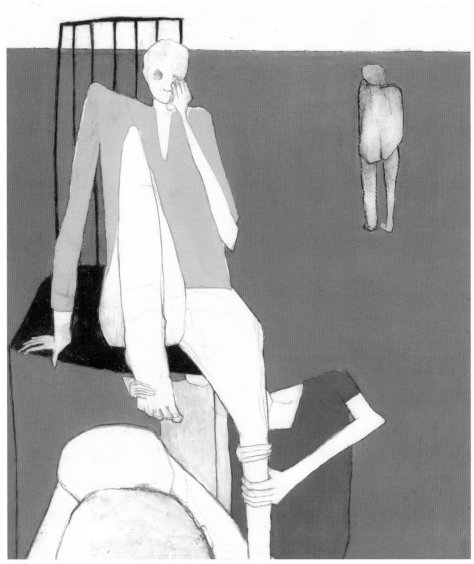

419

420

421

422

423

424
Artist: **Adam Rogers**
Medium: Digital
Size: 7" h x 6" w

425
Artist: **John H. Howard**
Medium: Acrylic on paper
Size: 30" h x 22" w

426
Artist: **Greg Tucker**
Medium: Pastel on paper
Size: 13" h x 9" w

427
Artist: **Jonathon Rosen**
Medium: Digital
Size: 8" h x 11" w

424

425

426

427

428
Artist: **James Bennett**
Medium: Oil on masonite
Size: 36" h x 48" w

429
Artist: **Darren Thompson**
Medium: Casein on gessoed panel
Size: 18" h x 14" w

430
Artist: **Mark Summers**
Medium: Scratchboard
Size: 12" h x 8" w

431
Artist: **Matthew D. Leake**
Medium: Scratchboard
Size: 11" h x 6" w

432
Artist: **Owen Smith**
Medium: Oil on canvas
Size: 36" h x 72" w

428

429

430

431

432

433
Artist: **Nicholas Wilton**

434
Artist: **Shane Rebenschied**
Art Director: Dean Sebring
Client: Miami New Times
Medium: Mixed, digital
Size: 12" h x 8" w

435
Artist: **Fred Otnes**
Art Director: Katie Marchese
Client: Reece Inc.
Medium: Mixed, collage on linen
Size: 60" h x 48" w

436
Artist: **Will Wilson**
Medium: Oil on canvas
Size: 9" h x 7" w

437
Artist: **Laura Goetz**
Medium: Watercolor on paper
Size: 12" h x 9" w

433

434

435

436

437

438
Artist: **M. Allen**
Medium: Oil, collage on board
Size: 21" h x 18" w

439
Artist: **Chris Spollen**
Client: Moonlight Press
Medium: Digital
Size: 14" h x 10" w

440
Artist: **Michael Whelan**
Client: Tree's Place Gallery
Medium: Acrylic on panel

441
Artist: **John Collier**
Medium: Pastel, watercolor on paper
Size: 20" h x 14" w

438

439

440

441

442
Artist: **John Collier**
Medium: Pastel, watercolor on paper
Size: 20" h x 14" w

443
Artist: **Gregory Manchess**
Medium: Oil on canvas

444
Artist: **John Vogt**
Medium: Acrylic on masonite
Size: 24" h x 24" w

445
Artist: **Dick Krepel**

446
Artist: **Jon Foster**
Medium: Oil on board
Size: 39" h x 30" w

442

443

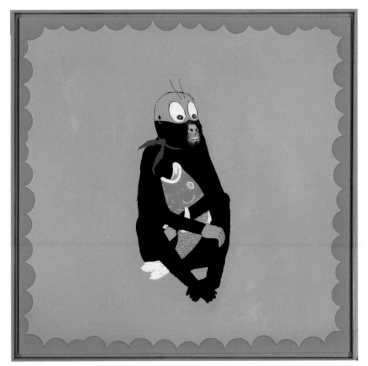

444

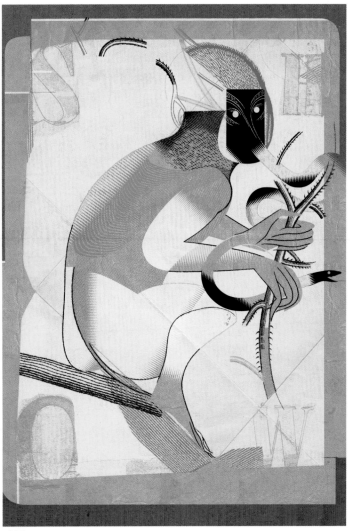

445

446

447
Artist: **Jon Foster**
Medium: Oil on board
Size: 39" h x 30" w

448
Artist: **Leo Espinosa**
Medium: Digital
Size: 5" h x 5" w

449
Artist: **James Tsukuda**
Medium: Pen & ink on board

450
Artist: **Mirko Ilic**
Medium: Digital
Size: 13" h x 10" w

451
Artist: **Brett Emanuel**
Medium: Digital
Size: 11" h x 8" w

447

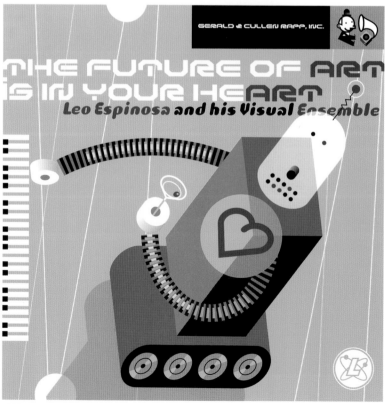

448

449

450

451

452
Artist: **Gary Taxali**
Medium: Alkyd on masonite
Size: 24" h x 32" w

453
Artist: **Gary Taxali**
Medium: Alkyd on masonite
Size: 24" h x 32" w

454
Artist: **Carolyn Fisher**
Medium: Acrylic, digital
Size: 12" h x 12" w

455
Artist: **Gary Baseman**
Medium: Acryic on canvas
Size: 24" h x 18" w

456
Artist: **Satoshi Kambayashi**
Medium: Digital
Size: 12" h x 8" w

452

453

454

455

456

457
Artist: **B. Royalty**
Medium: Gouache on Arches paper
Size: 22" h x 30" w

458
Artist: **Jessie Hartland**
Medium: Gouache on paper
Size: 11" h x 15" w

459
Artist: **Paul Cox**
Medium: Watercolor on paper
Size: 26" h x 20" w

460
Artist: **Miriam Shenitzer**
Medium: Etching, watercolor on paper
Size: 9" h x 9" w

461
Artist: **Christopher Nielsen**
Medium: Acrylic on wood
Size: 9" h x 5" w

457

458

459

460

461

STUDENT SCHOLARSHIP COMPETITION

The Society of Illustrators fulfills its education mission through its museum exhibitions, library, archives, permanent collection and, most proudly, through the Student Scholarship Competition.

The following pages present a sampling of the 110 works selected from over 5,200 entries from 69 schools submitted by college level students nationwide. The selections were made by a prestigious jury of professional illustrators.

Tim O'Brien chairs this program, and major financial support is given by Hallmark Corporation Foundation of Kansas City, Missouri. Along with donations from corporations, bequests, and an annual auction of member-donated works, the Society awards over $100,000 to the students and their institutions.

This year, Tom Allen and Barron Storey were selected as Distinguished Educators in the Arts, an honor now recognized by all as affirmation of an influential career in the classroom.

As you will see, the talent is there. If it is coupled with determination, these students will move ahead in this annual to join the selected professionals. Let's see.

HALLMARK CORPORATE FOUNDATION

Hallmark Corporate Foundation
Matching Grants

The Hallmark Corporate Foundation of Kansas City, Missouri, is again this year supplying full matching grants for all of the awards in the Society's Student Scholarship Competition. Grants, restricted to the Illustration Departments, are awarded to the following institutions:

11,500	School of Visual Arts
11,000	Art Center College of Design
5,000	Academy of Art College
5,000	Montserrat College of Art
3,000	Rhode Island School of Design
3,000	Syracuse University
2,000	Art Institute of Southern California
2,000	California College of Arts & Crafts
2,000	Pratt Institute
1,500	San Jose State University
1,000	American Academy of Art
1,000	California State University-Long Beach
1,000	Fashion Institute of Technology
1,000	Rocky Mountain College of Art and Design

SCHOLARSHIP COMMITTEE AND JURY

Committee

Tim O'Brien, *Chairman*
Lisa Cyr
Tim Bower
Lauren Uram
Kenneth Smith

Jury

Juliette Borda, illustrator
Cynthia Von Buhler, illustrator
Jim Burke, illustrator
Margaret Cusack, illustrator
Leonard Everett Fisher, illustrator
Fred Harper, illustrator
David Hollenbach, illustrator
Sari Levy, artists' representative
Scott Menchin, illustrator
Andrea Mistretta, illustrator

Eric Palma, illustrator
Roberto Parada, illustrator
David Ricceri, illustrator
Chris Sharpe, illustrator
Bruce Strachan, illustrator
Glynnis Sweeney, illustrator
Kristen Ulv, illustrator
Ellen Weinstein, illustrator
Eric White, illustrator
Lazar Zohar, illustrator

STUDENT SCHOLARSHIP COMPETITION

TOM ALLEN

I met Tom for the first time six years ago when he became the chairman of our illustration department here at Ringling School of Art and Design. Through Tom's work and friendship, it seems like I've known him forever. His homespun manner envelops this man of great curiosity and wisdom that touches all he encounters. This *Legendary Trail Blazer of Illustration* has always taken the time to give back so much to his profession through the classroom.

The impact of Tom's legendary teaching history spans over 40 years from the School of Visual Arts' first illustration courses to the formation of Syracuse's Masters programs in Illustration and Graphic Design. The educator, Tom Allen, has had an academic impact of enormous proportions.

The list of his past students reads like a Who's Who of illustration.

His teaching technique is to approach each student as an individual and to bring out his or her personal strengths. This pedagogy and his openness are the keys to his great success. He always welcomes the new, yet embraces the formalities of tradition. These are the characteristics of great leaders, thinkers and educators, all of which are Tom Allen.

Regan Todd Dunnick

BARRON STOREY

Barron Storey is a real teacher. I say this with great admiration and some envy. Seven years ago when I accepted the offer to chair the Illustration Department at the California College of Arts and Crafts, the first call I made was to Barron. I had heard he had recently resigned from a local art school in principled high dudgeon. This is nothing new: Barron is nothing if not passionately committed when it comes to teaching his vocation, illustration. I begged him to come out of his self-imposed retirement and help me build a decent program. After asking a lot of questions and extracting from me some commitments of my own, he accepted.

I have since told the school's administration, the students, our faculty, and him, many times, that I might be able to run the department without him, but I sure as hell wouldn't want to. He keeps the students alert and excited and the department honest. In fact if not quite in title, I'm exceedingly proud that he's my co-chair.

This is who he is: Whenever I hang out at the bar in the Society of Illustrators building in New York and we're telling war stories and such, if I mention Barron as my colleague at CCAC, I am immediately surrounded by people saying with pride, "Barron was my teacher." And they say it the way a cellist might say, "Pablo Casals was my teacher." Never mind that they had a dozen or so other teachers during their college days, Barron had clearly made the biggest impact on them. We then have a fine time telling each other wildly improbable Storey stories on into the night.

Legend is a wildly overused word. It's misapplied to one-hit wonders and ephemeral commodities, so I hesitate to use the word, even when it applies. Nevertheless, as an illustrator and mentor, to me as well as hundreds of our colleagues, Barron Storey is a truly legendary example.

Dugald Stermer

This annual award is selected by the Board of Directors upon recommendation of the Education Committee.
Past recipients: Alvin J. Pimsler 1997, Alan E. Cober 1998, Murray Tinkelman 1999, Marshall Arisman and Phillip Hays 2000

Jebediah E. Riley
Elissa Della-Piana, Instructor
Montserrat College of Art
$5,000 The Starr Foundation Award

Jeff Soto
Daniel Limrite, Instructor
Art Center College of Design
$4,000 Robert H. Blattner Award

Benjamin J. Blatt
Lenny Long/Mary Jane Begin,
Instructors
Rhode Island School of Design
$3,000 The Starr Foundation Award

Daniel Dos Santos
Marvin Mattelson, Instructor
School of Visual Arts
$3,000 Jellybean Photographics Award

Jan Descartes
Roger DeMuth, Instructor
Syracuse University
$3,000 Albert Dorne Award

Max Miceli
David Mocarski, Instructor
Art Center College of Design
$3,000 Albert Dorne Award
2002 "Call For Entries" Poster Award

Andrew De Graff
Rudy Gutierrez, Instructor
Pratt Institute
$2,000 Jellybean
Photographics Award

Maria E. Castro
David Limrite, Instructor
Art Center College of Design
$2,000 Kirchoff/Wohlberg Award

Moby Francke
William Maughan, Instructor
Academy of Art College
$3,000 The Starr Foundation Award

Cindy Eun Young Kim
Aaron Smith, Instructor
Art Center College of Design
$2,000 Award in Memory of
Helen Wohlberg Lambert

Maya Gohill
William Maughan, Instructor
Academy of Art College
$2,000 Award in Memory of
Herman Lambert

Michael Savas
George Zebot, Instructor
Art Institute of Southern California
$2,000 The Greenwich Workshop Award

Robert Donnelly
Francis Jetter, Instructor
School of Visual Arts
$1,000 The Wright Foundation
for the Arts Award

Arvin Luke Maala
Marvin Mattelson, Instructor
School of Visual Arts
$2,000 Jellybean Photographics Award

Caitlin Kuhwald
Dugald Stermer, Instructor
California College of Arts and Crafts
$2,000 Award in Memory of
Meg Wohlberg

Steve Zmina
Courtney Granner/Alize Canton,
Instructors
San Jose State University
$1,500 The Norman Rockwell
Museum at Stockbridge Award

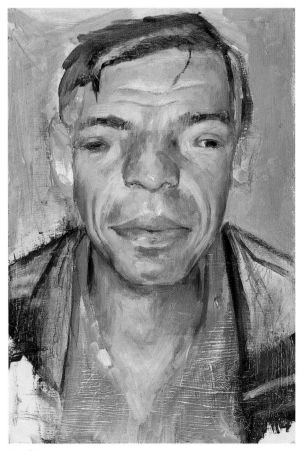

Marilyn Patrizio
Sal Catalano, Instructor
School of Visual Arts
$1,500 Dick Blick Art Materials Award
RSVP Publication Award

James Jean
Thomas Woodruff, Instructor
School of Visual Arts
$1,500 Award in Memory
of Alan M. Goffman

Bradley Silverman
Erik Aloescher, Instructor
School of Visual Arts
$1,500 The Norman Rockwell Museum at
Stockbridge Award

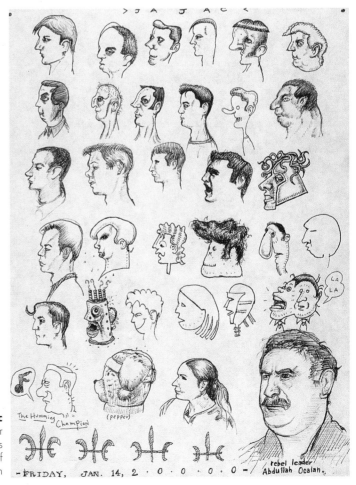

James Jajac
Robert Goldstrom, Instructor
School of Visual Arts
$1,000 Award in Memory of
Harry Rosenbaum

Matt Puentes
George Zebot, Instructor
California State University-Long Beach
$1,000 The Starr Foundation Award

Magda Smarzewska
Dr. John Trapp, Instructor
American Academy of Art
$1,000 Norma and Alvin Pimsler Award

Javier Poot
Mathew McFarren, Instructor
Rocky Mountain College of Art and Design
$1,000 Kirchoff/Wohlberg Award in Memory of
Frances Means

Komaki Yamakawa
Kam Mak, Instructor
Fashion Institute of Technology
$1,000 Award in Memory of Effie B. Bowie

Anna Cangialosi
Gil Ashby, Instructor
Center for Creative Studies

Rachel Jaksich Cox
Ken Krofcheck, Instructor
Maryland Institute,
College of Art

Machiyo Kodaira
Wendy Popp,
Instructor
Parsons School
of Design

Mark Bodnar
Anita Dawson, Instructor
Columbus College of Art & Design

Andrew R. Alley
Michael Carnige, Instructor
Art Institute of Fort Lauderdale

Robert Caldwell
Alex Bostic, Instructor
Virginia Commonwealth University

Allan Chow
Mark Schuler, Instructor
Kansas City Art Institute

Sean McGaghey
Robert Olsen, Instructor
Pikes Peak Community College

Jon Luna
Durwin Talon, Instructor
Savannah College of Art and Design

Cheryl Zamulinsky
Marty Blake, Instructor
Syracuse University

Michael Brasel
Tom Garrett, Instructor
Minneapolis College of Art and Design

Carrie Bolger
Peter Caras, Instructor
DuCret School of Art

Elizabeth Benson
Robert Barrett, Instructor
Brigham Young University

Lauren Bair
Patrick Fiore, Instructor
Ringling School of Art

Spring Hofeldt
John Lynch, Instructor
Central Missouri State University

Tiffany Gobler
John McDonald, Instructor
Kendall College of Art and Design

Meghan Fahey
Jim Edwards/Paul Olson, Instructors
Massachusetts College of Art

ARTISTS INDEX

DuBois, Gerard, 9
17 Pl Du Soleil #302
Verdun, Quebec
CANADA H3E 1P7
(514) 762-5043
rep (609) 252-9405
www.gdubois.com

Dunnick, Regan Todd, 422
7663 Peninsular Dr.
Sarasota, FL 34231
(941) 923-4751

Duvivier, Jean-Manuel, 97, 299, 369
c/o Daniele Collignon
200 West 15th St.
New York, NY 10011
(212) 243-4209
www.DanieleCollignon.Reps.com

Ehlert, Lois, 173
839 North Marshall St.
Milwaukee, WI 53202
(414) 276-8336
rep (212) 644-2020

Emanuel, Brett, 451
1212 West 8th St.
Kansas City, MO 64101
(913) 485-7490

Espinosa, Leo, 96, 102, 448
108 East 35th St.
New York, NY 10016
rep (212) 889-3337
www.theispot.com/artist/espinosa

Evilla, Josue R., 420
446 Hillside Ave.
Hartford, CT 06106
(860) 560-0617

Fancher, Lou, 169
Johnson & Fancher Inc.
440 Sheridan Ave. South
Minneapolis, MN 55405
(612) 377-8728

Fasolino, Teresa, 335
233 East 21st St. #6
New York, NY 10010
(212) 533-5543
rep (212) 989-4600
www.newborngroup.com

Fennimore, Linda, 234, 235, 237
808 West End Ave. #801
New York, NY 10025
(212) 866-0279

Fisher, Carolyn, 454
1815 24th Ave. NW
Calgary, Alberta
CANADA T2M 1Z3
(877) 712-8903
www.carolynfisher.com

Fisher, Jeffrey, 95, 179
c/o Riley Illustration
155 West 15th St. #4C
New York, NY 10011
(212) 989-8770

Foster, Jon, 446, 447
118 Everett Ave.
Providence, RI 02906
(401) 277-0880
www.jonfoster.com

Fraser, Douglas, 221
1161 Camrose Crescent
Victoria, BC
CANADA V8P 1M9
(250) 385-4881

Frazier, Craig, 93, 94, 380
381, 382
90 Throckmorton Ave. #28
Mill Valley, CA 94941
(415) 389-1475
www.craigfrazier.com

Frazier, Jim, 88, 376, 413
221 Lakeridge Dr.
Dallas, TX 75218
(214) 340-9972

French, Lisa, 229, 398
355 Molino Ave.
Long Beach, CA 90814
(562) 434-5277

Gadino, Victor, 270
417 East 90th St. #3D
New York, NY 10128
(212) 860-8066 fax (212) 534-4650

Gall, Chris, 86, 291, 318, 343, 345
4421 North Camino del Santo
Tucson, AZ 85718
(520) 299-4454
www.chrisgall.com

Gast, Josef, 392
rep (740) 369-9702
www.sturgesreps.com

George, Josh, 324
990 Bushwick Ave. #2C
Brooklyn, NY 11221
(718) 919-2172

Gibbs, Michael, 360
13908 Stonefield Lane
Clifton, VA 20124
(703) 502-3400
www.michaelgibbs.com

Giusti, Robert, 337
170 Skyline Ridge Rd.
Bridgewater, CT 06752
(860) 354-6539
rep (212) 989-4600
www.newborngroup.com

Goetz, Laura, 437
46 Elm St.
Islip, NY 11751
(631) 277-5133

Goines, David Lance, 282, 286,
288, 320
St. Hieronymus Press
1703 MLK
Berkeley, CA 94709
(510) 549-1405
www.goines.net

Gore, Leonid, 148
1429 Dahill Rd. Apt. A
Brooklyn, NY 11204
(718) 627-4952
rep (212) 675-5719

Grafe, Max, 58
99 Sutton St. #302
Brooklyn, NY 11222
(718) 609-0340
rep (212) 687-6463

GrandPré, Mary, 301
597 Pascal St. South
St. Paul, MN 55116
(651) 699-0424

Greif, Gene, 87
114 West 16th St. #6E
New York, NY 10011
(212) 647-1286
rep (212) 889-3337

Grossman, Robert, 26
19 Crosby St.
New York,, NY 1965

Guarnaccia, Steven, 79, 98, 198, 199
31 Fairfield St.
Montclair, NJ 07042
(973) 746-9785

Gustafson, Mats, 2
c/o Art & Commerce
755 Washington St.
New York, NY 10014
(212) 206-0737 fax (212) 989-6462

Gutierrez, Rudy, 271, 289
330 Haven Ave. #1D
New York, NY 10033
(212) 568-2848

Hansson, Riber, 44
Garvargatan 5
Stockholm, SWEDEN
468-650-8884

Hanuka, Tomer, 110, 114
449 Grand St. #2L
Brooklyn, NY 11211
(718) 963-3383

Hargis, Kris, 370, 371
c/o Levy Creative Management
300 East 46th St. #4G
New York, NY 10017
(212) 687-6463

Hartland, Jessie, 241, 458
165 William St.
New York, NY 10038
(212) 233-1413
www.jessiehartland.com

Hartung, Susan Kathleen, 157
(517) 592-5402
www.susanhartung.com

Helquist, Brett, 54, 170
516 East 88th St. #1A
New York, NY 10128
(212) 517-9076
rep (212) 333-2551
www.shannonassociates.com

Helton, Linda, 372
7000 Meadow Lake
Dallas, TX 75214
(214) 319-7877
rep (609) 252-9405

Henderson, Stephanie, 272
c/o Fran Seigel
160 West End Ave. #23-S
New York, NY 10023
(212) 486-9644
www.fsartists.com

Hewgill, Jody, 53, 57, 213,
273, 274, 411
260 Brunswick Ave.
Toronto, Ontario
CANADA M5S 2M7
(416) 924-4200
www.jodyhewgill.com

Hirschfeld, Al, 35, 39
c/o Feiden Galleries
699 Madison Ave.
New York, NY 10021
(212) 223-4230

Ho, David, 73
3586 Dickenson Common
Fremont, CA 94538
(510) 656-2468

Holland, Brad, 306, 367,
368, 402, 410
96 Greene St.
New York, NY 10012
(212) 226-3675 fax (212) 941-5520

Hollenbach, David, 317
rep (740) 369-9702
www.sturgesreps.com

Holley, Jason, 59, 64
391 West Grandview Ave.
Sierra Madre, CA 91024
(626) 355-7969

Hood, William, 366
(740) 369-9702
www.sturgesreps.com

Howard, John H., 215, 386, 388,
389, 425
c/o The Newborn Group
115 West 23rd St. #43A
New York, NY 10011
(212) 989-4600 fax (212) 989-8998
www.newborngroup.com

Huynh, Phung, 412
(740) 369-9702
www.sturgesreps.com

Ilic, Mirko, 450
207 East 32nd St.
New York, NY 10016
(212) 481-9737

Isip, Jordin, 120
536 5th St. #2
Brooklyn, NY 11215
(718) 499-0985
www.jordinisip.com

Jackson, Jeff, 116, 168
92 Bedford Rd.
Toronto, Ontario
CANADA M5R 2K2
(416) 972-6468

Jarrie, Martin, 216
c/o Marlena Agency
145 Witherspoon St.
Princeton, NJ 08542
(609) 252-9405

Jetter, Frances, 151
2211 Broadway
New York, NY 10024
(212) 580-3720

Johnson, Stephen T., 364
1329 Inverness
Lawrence, KS 66049
(785) 312-9767
rep (212) 223-9545

Johnson, Steve, 169
Johnson & Fancher Inc.
440 Sheridan Ave. South
Minneapolis, MN 55405
(612) 377-8728

Jones, Douglas, 417
c/o Gerald & Cullen Rapp
108 East 35th St. #1
New York, NY 10016
(212) 889-3337
gerald@rappart.com
www.douglasbjones.com

Joyce, William, 197
3302 Centenary Blvd.
Shreveport, LA 71104
(318) 869-0180
rep (310) 472-0245

Juhasz, Victor, 27
576 Westminster Ave.
Elizabeth, NJ 07208
(908) 351-4227 fax (908) 355-0179
rep (212) 989-4600

Kambayashi, Satoshi, 456
a.k.a. Paquebot
Flat 2, 40 Tisbury Rd.
Hove, East Sussex, UK BN3 3BA
(011) 44-1273-771539
www.satoshi-illustration.com

Karas, G. Brian, 191
97 Lamoree Rd.
Rhinebeck, NY 12572
(845) 876-0857

Kascht, John, 36, 38
2401 Fairview Dr.
Alexandria, VA 22306
(703) 768-8370

Kelley, Gary, 20, 217, 220, 281,
  313, 315
226 1/2 Main St.
Cedar Falls, IA 50613
(319) 277-2330 fax (319) 268-2214
rep (212) 223-9545

Kimber, Murray, 226, 385
c/o Richard Solomon Artists Rep.
305 East 50th St. #1
New York, NY 10022
(212) 223-9545 fax (212) 223-9633

Krepel, Dick, 445
869 Warnell Dr.
Richmond Hill, GA 31324
(912) 727-3368
rkrepel@earthlink.net

Kunz, Anita, 24, 29, 49, 218
218 Ontario St.
Toronto, Ontario
CANADA M5A 2V5
(416) 364-3846 fax (416) 368-3947
www.anitakunz.com

Laden, Nina, 115
6750 26th Ave. NW
Seattle, WA 98117
rep (631) 286-1278 (children's books)
rep (206) 232-7873

Leake, Matthew D., 431
302 Bethel Ave.
Aston, PA 19014
(610) 497-5903

Leonard, Gabe, 407
3725 Nicolet Ave. #1
Los Angeles, CA 90016
(800) 880-4770
www.gabeleonard.com

Lesh, David, 374
5693 North Meridian St.
Indianapolis, IN 46208
(317) 253-3141

Lessard, Marie, 139
4641 Hutchison
Montreal, Quebec
CANADA H2V 4A2
(514) 272-5696 fax (514) 272-3494

Levine, Laura, 121, 122, 123
444 Broome St.
New York, NY 10013
(212) 431-4787

Lewin, Betsy, 188
152 Willoughby Ave.
Brooklyn, NY 11205
(718) 622-3882 fax (718) 398-9557

Locke, Gary, 344
2702 S. FR. 227
Rogersville, MO 65742
(417) 823-8650

Long, Loren, 177, 266, 354,
  355, 393
5839 Owl Nest Dr.
West Chester, OH 45069
(513) 942-4551
rep (212) 223-9545

Lorenz, Albert, 260, 333
49 Pine Ave.
Floral Park, NY 11001
(516) 354-5530 fax (516) 328-8864

MacDonald, Ross, 99
56 Castle Meadow Rd.
Newtown, CT 06470
(203) 270-6438

Manchess, Grgeory, 307, 331, 443
13358 SW Gallop Ct.
Portland, OR 97008-7282
(503) 590-5447 fax (503) 590-6331
rep (212) 223-9545

Marten, Ruth, 37
8 West 13th St. #7RW
New York, NY 10011
(212) 645-0233

Martinez, Ricardo, 61
c/ Condado de Trevino 2-13G
Madrid, SPAIN 28033
(3491) 5864855

Masuda, Coco, 201, 232, 233, 236
40 Harrison St. #4M
New York, NY 10013
(212) 732-2599
www.cocomasuda.com

Matcho, Mark, 200
70 Harkness Ave. #9
Pasadena, CA 91106
(626) 796-6906

Mayer, Bill, 214, 304, 351
240 Forkner Dr.
Decatur, GA 30030
(404) 378-0686

McCauley, Adam, 108, 182, 183,
  206, 242
2400 8th Ave.
Oakland, CA 94606
(510) 832-0860
rep (415) 641-1285
www.atomicalley.com

McKean, Dave, 13, 117, 119
c/o Allen Spiegel Fine Arts
221 Lobos Ave.
Pacific Grove, CA 93950
(831) 372-4672

McKowen, Scott, 228, 230, 259
428 Downie St.
Stratford, Ontario
CANADA N5A 1X7
(519) 271-3049
rep (609) 252-9405
www.marlenaagency.com

McLean, Wilson, 332, 336, 384
41 West Court St.
Hudson, NY 12534
(518) 828-3484
www.newborngroup.com

McMullan, James, 10, 15
207 East 32nd St.
New York, NY 10016
(212) 689-5527 fax (212) 689-4522

Meganck, Robert, 14
1 North 5th St. #500
Richmond, VA 23219-2231
(804) 644-9200
rep (412) 761-5666
www.robert@meganck.com

Meisel, Paul, 164
2 Pheasant Ridge Rd.
Newtown, CT 06470
(203) 270-6692
rep (212) 675-5719

Milelli, Pascal, 147, 302, 308
402 West Pender St. #609
Vancouver, BC
CANADA V6B 1T6
(604) 608-2708 fax (604) 682-6086

Minor, Wendell, 136, 309
P.O. Box 1135
Washington, CT 06793
(860) 868-9101 fax (860) 868-9512
www.minorart.com

Montgomery, Linda, 314
Brookfield Farm Studio
RR #1
Alliston, Ontario
CANADA L9R 1V1
(705) 435-3022
www.theispot.com/artist/lmontgomery

Moore, Larry, 219, 222, 276
1315 Edgewater Dr.
Orlando, FL 32804
(407) 648-0832

Myers, Lou, 109
58 Lakeview Ave. West
Cortlandt Manor, NY 10566
(914) 737-2307

Nagasawa, Eriko, 305
Media Co., Ltd.
3-11 Umegae-cho
Gifu, JAPAN 500-8818
(81) 58-262-9912

Nakata, Hiroe, 166, 167
328 West 17th St. #2R
New York, NY 10011
(212) 647-9178
rep (212) 675-5719

Nascimbene, Yan, 180, 322
235 7th St.
Davis, CA 95616
(530) 756-7076

Nash, Scott, 196
88 Welch St.
Peaks Island, ME 04108
(207) 766-5761

Nelson, Kadir, 72, 160
P.O. Box 262488
San Diego, CA 92196-2488
(888) 310-3222
www.kadirnelson.com

Neubecker, Robert, 89, 243
505 East 3rd Ave.
Salt Lake City, UT 84103
(801) 531-6999 fax (801) 531-6868

Nielsen, Christopher, 461
7/9 Miller St. Bondi
Sydney, NSW, AUSTRALIA 2026
0412-563-024
www.illosight.com.au

Niklewicz, Adam, 66
44 Great Quarter Rd.
Sandy Hook, CT 06482
(203) 270-8424

Nobriga, Jason, 414
1212 8th Ave. #8
Honolulu, HI 96816
(808) 381-9913

Northeast, Christian, 100
336 Rusholme Rd. Upper Fl.
Toronto, Ontario
CANADA M6H 2Z5
(416) 538-0400

Noruzi, Charlotte, 178
Question Design
510 East 79th St. #1F
New York, NY 10021
(212) 639-1988
rep (212) 333-2551

O'Brien, Tim, 33, 46
310 Marlborogh Rd.
Brooklyn, NY 11226
(718) 282-2821 fax (718) 282-1843
www.obrienillustration.com

O'Connell, Eileen, 146
256 Belleville Ave. #B3
Belleville, NJ 07109
(973) 844-1621

Olbinski, Rafal, 181, 267, 268, 269
142 East 35th St.
New York, NY 10016
(212) 532-4328 fax (212) 532-4348

Olivere, Raymond, 330
1435 Lexington Ave.
New York, NY 10128
(212) 534-0852 fax (212) 831-0598

Orosz, Istvan, 310
c/o Marlena Agency
145 Witherspoon St.
Princeton, NJ 08542
(609) 252-9405

PROFESSIONAL STATEMENTS

Jack Harris
Illustration

722 Yorklyn Road,
Suite 150
Hockessin, DE 19707

www.jackharris.com
Studio
302-477-1689

JACK HARRIS • 302-477-1689

Illustration makes the invisible

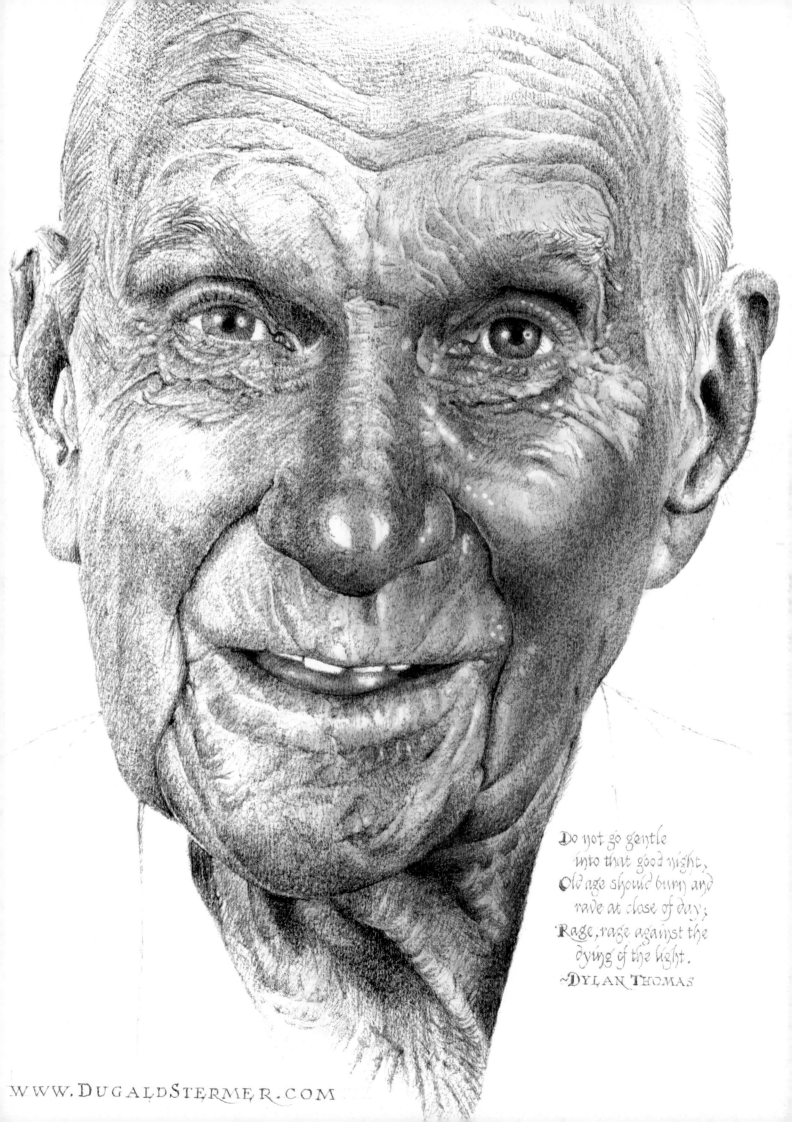

Do not go gentle
into that good night,
Old age should burn and
rave at close of day;
Rage, rage against the
dying of the light.
~DYLAN THOMAS

www.DugaldStermer.com

Great illustrators represent Gerald & Cullen Rapp

Beth Adams

Philip Anderson

N. Ascencios

Stuart Briers

Lonnie Busch

Jonathan Carlson

R. Gregory Christie

Jack Davis

Robert de Michiell

The Dynamic Duo

Randall Enos

Leo Espinosa

Phil Foster

Mark Fredrickson

Eliza Gran

Gene Greif

Peter Horjus

Peter Horvath

Celia Johnson

Douglas Jones

James Kaczman

Steve Keller

J.D. King

Laszlo Kubinyi

Scott Laumann

Davy Liu

PJ Loughran

Hal Mayforth

David McLimans

Aaron Meshon

James O'Brien

John Pirman

Jean-Francois Podevin

Marc Rosenthal

Alison Seiffer

Seth

Whitney Sherman

Jeffrey Smith

James Steinberg

Drew S.

Elizabeth Traynor

Anders Wenngren

Michael Witte

Noah Woods

Brad Yeo

And **Gerald & Cullen Rapp** has represented great illustrators since 1944

108 East 35th Street, New York, NY 10016 | Phone 212 889 3337 | Fax 212 889 3341 | www.theispot.com/rep/rapp

PETER ANDREW

Peter Andrew Illustration
936 564-0201 • fax 936 468-4041
andrew@txucom.net

Represented by Susan Albert Athas
781 769-8011 • fax 781 769-0653
ftbf@aol.com

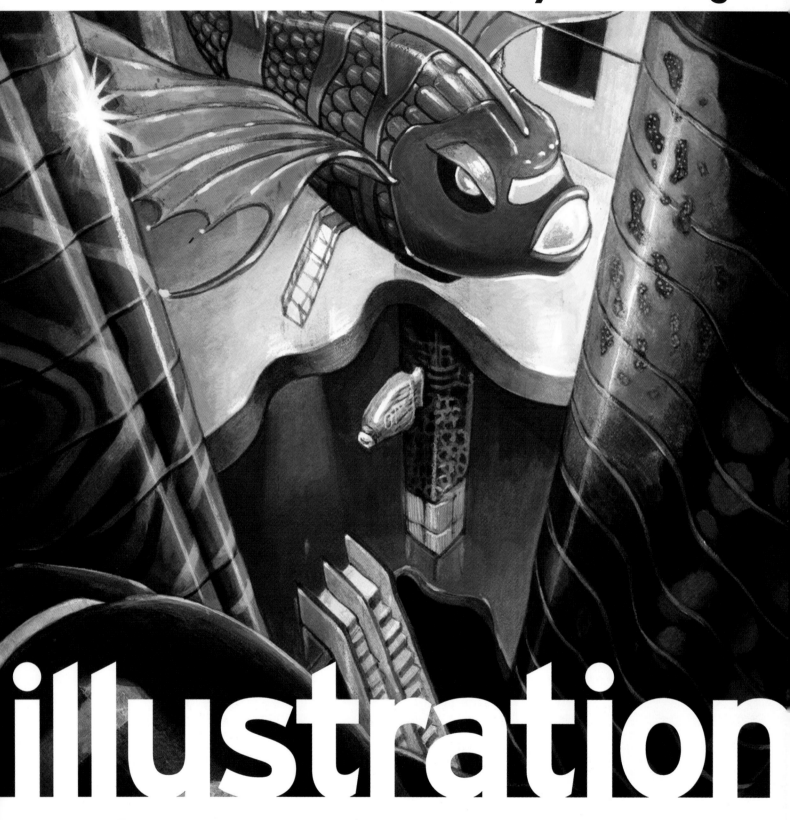

ALLEN DOUGLAS 718-499-4101

PATRICK MILBOURN

PORTRAITS

327 West 22 Street
New York, NY 10011
(212) 989-4594
www.theispot.com/artist/pmilbourn

MIKE DUBISCH

DUBISCHNY@AOL.COM
(845)626-4386

Michael Medau
1707 S. Main St.
Seattle, WA 98144
800.484.9670 x8833
michaelmedau.com

866 United Nations Plaza New York, New York 10017
Phone: 212-644-2020 Fax: 212-223-4387
www.kirchoffwohlberg.com

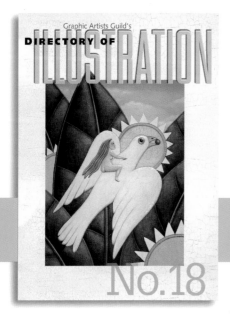

PAT BUCHANAN'S SHRINKING AMERICA   Philadelphia Weekly cover

RUDY'S SECRET   The Village Voice cover

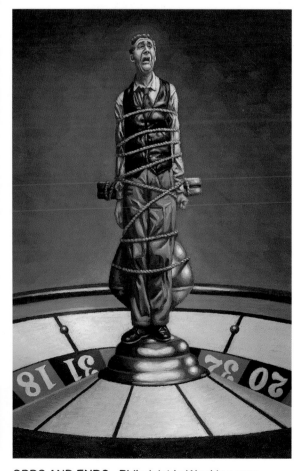

ODDS AND ENDS   Philadelphia Weekly cover

ROUGH RIDE   Barron's cover

GARY AAGAARD   (718) 694-0458   Fax (718) 923-1350   AAGZ@msn.com

SOCIETY ACTIVITIES

THE DAVID P. USHER/GREENWICH WORKSHOP
MEMORIAL AWARD

⸎

JON FOSTER

"Crowbot"

The selection was made from all of the works exhibited in the 42nd Annual. The jury included:
Past Medalists Natalie Ascenios and Kinuko Craft, Exhibition Chair Nancy Stahl
and representing The Greenwich Workshop, Scott Usher and Peter Landa.
A cash prize and subsequent print edition accompanies this award.

GreenwichWorkshop

THE WAIT IS OVER!

Phillip R.Goodwin

WE FINALLY PUT IN A WATER RIDE

We're lying. The roof leaks. But there are lots of real amusements that you'll experience when
you join the Society of Illustrators.

If you are a working Illustrator, you should be part of this organization. If you are a Designer,
Art Director, Art Educator or Illustrators Rep, you probably qualify in one of several associate
categories. Just Call the Society and we'll send you membership information.

Join now...before the dues are raised to pay for the Ferris Wheel.

Society of Illustrators
128 East 63rd Street
New York, NY 10021
212 838 2560

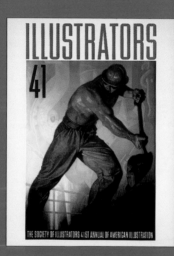
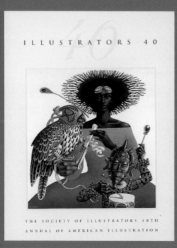
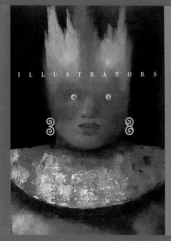

THE ILLUSTRATOR IN AMERI-CA 1860 - 2000

NEW EXPANDED EDITION!

BY WALT REED
EDITED BY ROGER REED

First published in 1964, this is the third edition of *The Illustrator in America*. It now goes back in time to the Civil War when artist reporters made on -the-spot pictures of the military action for publication by newspapers and periodicals of the day.

Following the improvements in printing and the attractions of better reproductions, the turn of the century brought a "Golden Age of Illustration" spearheaded by Howard Pyle, Edwin Austin Abbey, A.B. Frost and others, who brought it to a high art. Illustrators were celebrities along with the authors whose works they pictured.

This history of 140 years of illustration is brought up to the millennium year of 2000 when the new computer-generated techniques and digital printing is creating another revolution in this evolving, dynamic art form.

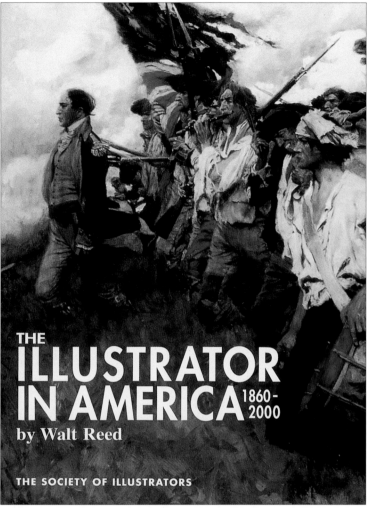

As before, the pictures and biographies of the outstanding artists of each decade are presented along with the historical context of each ten-year period. A time-line chart presents the various influences of styles, schools, and "isms" within this diverse and vital field that has made such an important contribution to America's art.

Included are the works of over 650 artists, their biographies, examples of their signatures and their best works. Among the artists are Winslow Homer, Thomas Moran, Charles Dana Gibson, Frederic Remington, William Glackens, Maxfield Parrish, N.C. Wyeth, James Montgomery Flagg, J.C. and F.X. Leyendecker, Jessie Wilcox Smith, John Held Jr., Norman Rockwell, Dean Cornwell, John Falter, Harold von Schmidt, Stevan Dohanos, Robert Fawcett, Austin Briggs, Al Parker, Bernie Fuchs, Bob Peak, Brad Holland, Milton Glaser, Richard Amsel, Gary Kelley, Leo and Diane Dillon, and Chris Van Allsberg.

COVER ILLUSTRATION:
"The Nation Makers" by Howard Pyle
Collection of the Brandywine River Museum

458 PAGES, FULL COLOR, HARDBOUND.
$49.95

Fred Otnes

Guy Billout

Chris Spollen

Joan Hall

PRO-ILLUSTRATION
by Jill Bossert

A How-to Series
$24.00 EACH. SET OF TWO $40.00

VOLUME ONE
EDITORIAL ILLUSTRATION

The Society of Illustrators has simulated an editorial assignment for a Sunday magazine supplement surveying the topic of "Love." Topics assigned to the illustrators include: Erotic Love, First Love, Weddings, Sensual Love, Computer Love, Adultery and Divorce. The stages of execution. from initial sketch to finish, are shown in a series of photographs and accompanying text. It's a unique, behind-the-scenes look at each illustrator's studio and the secrets of their individual styles. Professional techniques demonstrated include oil, acrylic, collage, computer, etching, trompe l'oeil, dyes and airbrush.

EDITORIAL

Marshall Arisman, Guy Billout, Alan E. Cober, Elaine Duillo, Joan Hall, Wilson McLean, Barbara Nessim, Tim O'Brien, Mel Odom

VOLUME TWO
ADVERTISING ILLUSTRATION

This is an advertising campaign for a fictitious manufacturer of timepieces. The overall concept is "Time" and nine of the very best illustrators put their talents to solving the problem. The stages of execution, from initial phone call to finish, are described in photographs and text. You'll understand the demonstration of the techniques used to create a final piece of art. Professional techniques demonstrated include oil, acrylic, mixed media collage, computer, three-dimension and airbrush.

ADVERTISING

N. Ascencios, Mark Borow, Robert M. Cunningham, Teresa Fasolino, Mark Hess, Hiro Kimura, Rafal Olbinski, Fred Otnes, Chris Spollen

FAMOUS AMERICAN ILLUSTRATORS
by Arpi Ermoyan
THE HALL OF FAME

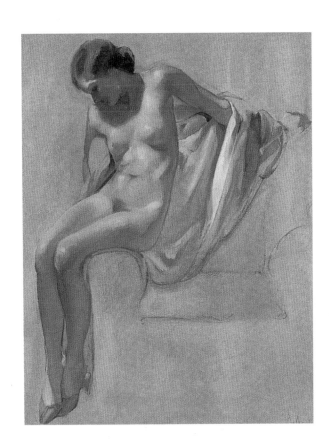

Every year since the inception of the Hall of Fame in 1958, the Society of Illustrators bestows its highest honor upon those artists recognized for their distinguished achievement in the art of illustration. The 87 recipients of the Hall of Fame Award represented in this book are the foremost illustrators of the last two centuries.

FAMOUS AMERICAN ILLUSTRATORS, a full-color, 224 page volume, is a veritable "Who's Who" of American illustration. The artists are presented in the order in which they were elected to the Hall of Fame. Included are short biographical sketches and major examples of each artist's work. Their range of styles is all-encompassing, their viewpoints varied, their palettes imaginative. The changing patterns of life in America are vividly recorded as seen through the eyes of these men and women—the greatest illustrators of the 19th and 20th Centuries. **11 1-2 x 12 inches. $34.95**

THE BUSINESS LIBRARY

Each of these volumes is a valuable asset to the professional artist whether established or just starting out. Together they form a solid base for your business.

HEALTH HAZARDS MANUAL
A comprehensive review of materials and supplies, from fixatives to pigments, airbrushes to solvents.
132 pages, softbound.
$9.95

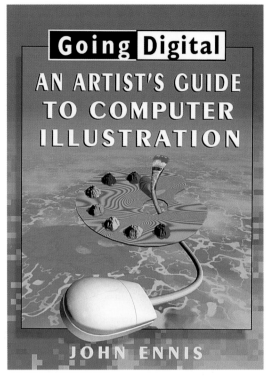

GOING DIGITAL
AN ARTIST'S GUIDE TO COMPUTER ILLUSTRATION
At last, an easy-to-read guide to illustrating on your computer. Author and illustrator, John Ennis, offers an under- the-hood look at how it's done and how to start up your digital studio.
144 pages, softbound, color.
$29.95

THE EDUCATION OF AN ILLUSTRATOR
Steve Heller and Marshall Arisman have assembled 20 top educators in essay and interview as to how graphic design/ illustration is taught and learned. Eight sample curricula are included.
288 pages, softcover, color.
$18.95

THE LEGAL GUIDE FOR THE VISUAL ARTIST
1999 EDITION.
Tad Crawford's text explains basic copyrights, moral rights, the sale of rights, taxation, business accounting and the legal support groups available to artists.
256 pages, softbound.
$19.95

GRAPHIC ARTISTS GUILD HANDBOOK
PRICING AND ETHICAL GUIDELINES -
VOL. 10
Includes an outline of ethical standards and business practices, as well as price ranges for hundreds of uses and sample contracts.
312 page, softbound.
$34.95

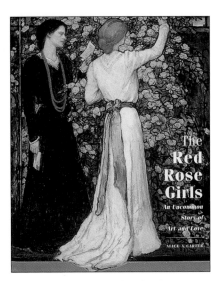

THE RED ROSE GIRLS
Jessie Willcox Smith, Elizabeth Shippen Green and Violet Oakley left Howard Pyle's school to become illustrators at the beginning of the last Century. They also lived together in "The Red Rose Inn" outside Philadelphia. Bunny Carter authored this edition. Cover by Violet Oakley.
216 pages, color, hardbound.
$39.95

DEAN CORNWELL
DEAN OF ILLUSTRATORS
The reissue of Pat Broder's 1978 biography, which has been long out of print. Cornwell was the prolific master draftsmen and consumate visual storyteller. Introductions by Norman Rockwell and Walt Reed.
240 pages, color, hardbound.
$70.00

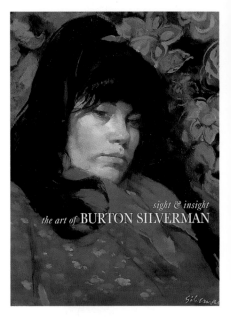

SIGHT & INSIGHT -
THE ART OF BURTON SILVERMAN
From the exhibition held at the Butler Institute of American Art in Youngstown, Ohio and the Brigham Young Museum in Provo, UT, 1999. This book is a collection of the past 25 years of work by this universally respected painter, illustrator and teacher.
157 pages, color, hardbound.
$39.95

BOOKS & CATALOGS

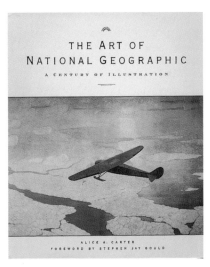

THE ART OF NATIONAL GEOGRAPHIC
A CENTURY OF ILLUSTRATION
175 images by 75 artists from the vast archives of the Geographic are presented by author, Bunny Carter, in six chapters: Anthropology, Discovery, Natural History, Conflict, The Universe and Cultures. Bios of the artists and a forward by Stephen Gould are included. Cover by N.C. Wyeth.
240 pages, color, hardbound. **$50.00**

ROLLING STONE:
THE ILLUSTRATED PORTRAITS
93 illustrators and 173 illustrated portraits from this magazine's over 35 years of covering the music scene have been assembled by current Art Director, Fred Woodward. Julian Allen to Janet Woolley. Muhammad Ali to Frank Zappa. Cover by Mark Ryden. 218 pages, color, hardbound. **$40.00**

JOHN LA GATTA - AN ARTIST'S LIFE
Hall of Fame illustrator John La Gatta lived a life as glamorous as the elegant men and gorgeous women he depicted during the twenties and thirties for magazines and advertisers. A biography and lavish portfolio of his work reveals one of the Golden Age's most famous artists.
168 pages, color, hardbound. **$39.95**
168 pages, color, paperback. **$29.95**

STILL AVAILABLE

WENDELL MINOR:
ART FOR THE WRITTEN WORD

$30.00

EDWARD SOREL:
UNAUTHORIZED PORTRAITS

$30.00

THE J.C. LEYENDECKER
COLLECTION

$16.00

COBY WHITMORE

$16.00

APPAREL

SI CAPS
Blue or Red with SI logo and name embroidered in white. Adjustable, one size fits all **$15.**

White shirt with the Society logo.
L, XL, XXL **$15.**

39TH ANNUAL EXHIBITION "CALL" T-SHIRT
Image of the tattooed face by Anita Kunz. 100% cotton. Heavyweight pocket T. Only XL, XXL **$15.**

38TH ANNUAL EXHIBITION "CALL" T-SHIRT
Image of a frog on a palette by Jack Unruh. Frog on front pocket. 100% cotton. Heavyweight pocket T. Only XL, XXL **$15.**

NAVY BLUE MICROFIBER NYLON CAP
SI logo and name embroidered in white. Floppy style cap. Feels broken in before its even worn. Adjustable, one size fits all.
$20.

SWEATSHIRTS
Blue with white lettering of multiple logos or grey with large red SI.
Blue L, XL, XXL **$20.**
Gray L, XL **$20.**

40TH ANNUAL EXHIBITION "CALL" T-SHIRT
Image of "The Messenger" by Leo and Diane Dillon. 100% cotton. Heavyweight pocket T. Only L, XXL **$15.**

GIFT ITEMS

SI LAPEL PINS
Actual Size
$6.00

The Society's
famous
Red and Black
logo, designed
by Bradbury
Thompson, is
featured on
many items.

SI TOTE BAGS
Heavyweight, white canvas bags are 14" high with the
two-color logo **$15.00**

SI PATCH
White with blue lettering
and piping - 4" wide
$4.00

SI CERAMIC COFFEE MUGS
Heavyweight 14 oz. mugs feature the
Society's logo or original illustrations
from the Permanent Collection.
1. John Held, Jr.'s "Flapper";
2. Norman Rockwell's "Dover Coach";
3. J. C. Leyendecker's "Easter";
4. Charles Dana Gibson's "Gibson Girl"
5. SI Logo
$6.00 each

SI NOTE CARDS
Norman Rockwell greeting cards, 3-7/8" x 8-5/8",
inside blank, great for all occasions.
Includes 100% rag envelopes

10 CARDS	**- $10.00**
20 CARDS	**- $18.00**
50 CARDS	**- $35.00**
100 CARDS	**- $60.00**

ORDER FORM

Mail: The Museum Shop, Society of Illustrators, 128 East 63rd Street, New York, NY 10021-7303
Phone: 1-800-SI-MUSEUM (1-800-746-8738)   Fax: 1-212-838-2561   EMail: SI1901@aol.com

43

NAME _____

COMPANY _____

STREET _____
(No P.O. Box numbers please)

CITY _____

STATE _____ ZIP _____

PHONE ( ) _____

Enclosed is my check for $ _____
Make checks payable to SOCIETY OF ILLUSTRATORS

Please charge my credit card:

❑ **American Express** ❑ **Master Card** ❑ **Visa**

CARD NUMBER _____

SIGNATURE _____ EXPIRATION DATE _____

*please note if name appearing on the card is different than the mailing name.

Ship via FEDEX Economy and charge my account _____

QTY	DESCRIPTION	SIZE	COLOR	PRICE	TOTAL

# of items ordered	

Total price of item(s) ordered	
TAX (NYS Residents add 8 1/4%)	
UPS Shipping per order	6.00
or **Foreign Shipping via Surface per order**	15.00
or **Foreign Shipping via Air per order**	CONTACT OFFICE
	FX
TOTAL DUE	